BRUCE LEE
The Biography
By Robert Clouse

UP UNIQUE
PUBLICATIONS

Photos courtesy of the Linda Lee family library, Robert Clouse, Dan Inosanto, Golden Harvest Studios, Warner Bros. Studios, *Inside Kung-Fu* magazine, *Inside Karate* magazine, George Foon, Steve Johnson, Doug Palmer, and Grace Lee.

Cover illustration: Penelope Gottlieb

ISBN: 0-86568-133-3
Library of Congress Catalog Card Number: 88-51058

Designer: Danilo J. Silverio
Editor: Dave Cater

UP UNIQUE PUBLICATIONS
4201 Vanowen Place
Burbank, CA 91505

Table of Contents

My direct contact with Bruce Lee occurred between November, 1972 and June, 1973 when I started preproduction of the film **Enter the Dragon** and through the post-production period when Bruce came to Warner Brothers Studios in Burbank, Calif., to complete some dubbing of dialogue that had been poorly recorded in Hong Kong. Many of the people I interviewed for this book I had known from that time, but many others I met for the first time during research of the elusive Bruce Lee. My perceptions of Lee were dented and bent from what I knew about him; others were destroyed. Trying to find an accurate and objective picture of another human being is the biographer's problem.

As an example, various police departments have conducted exercises that demonstrate how mixed can be the accounts of those witnessing an act that has just occurred. Six healthy people are seated to the rear of a room where, they are told, a particular act is about to unfold. A door opens and a man walks in to take a chair. Suddenly a man and a woman step into the room, the man carrying a gun, which he proceeds to fire at the man in the chair. The man slumps to the floor as the man and woman run from the room, using different exits. Not especially complicated. Quite clear-cut. But when the eyewitnesses are questioned by the police, a vastly divergent story emerges. It was the woman who was killed. The man did not have a gun, but a knife. They both left by the same door. The seated man was wearing a trench coat. No he wasn't. He was wearing a sports jacket.

Now take events that happened some years ago as witnessed by people of different cultures and different experiences and what comes forth becomes rather contradictory. An understatement. There are individuals who have a particular ax to grind, or wish to bury an episode that might prove embarrassing, or someone who feels protective of a public image. Piecing together the portrait is imprecise, but the attempt goes on.

--**Robert Clouse**

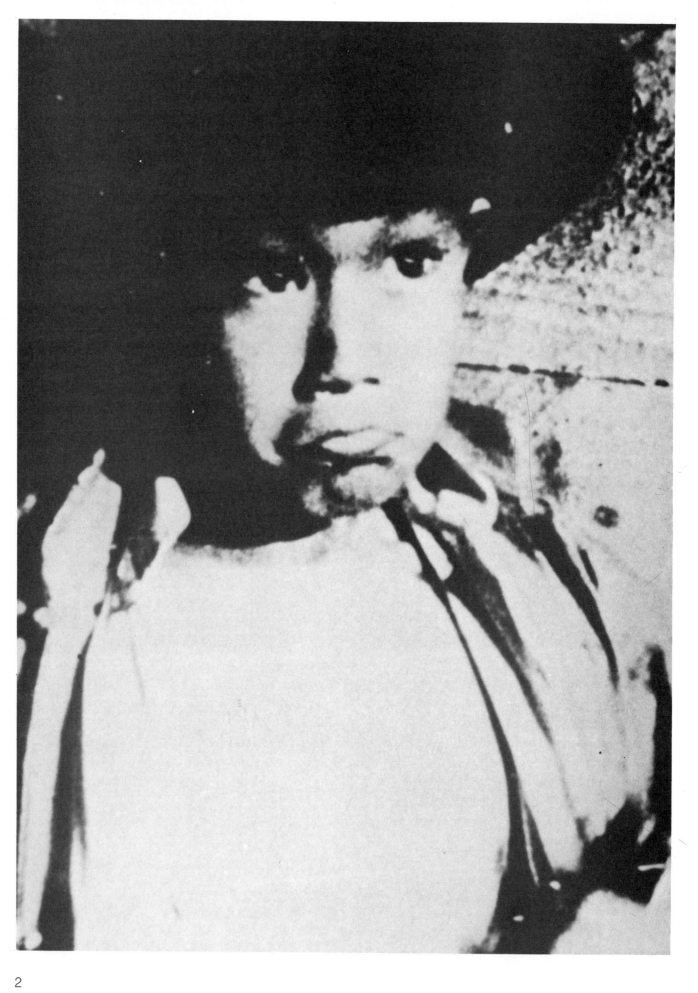

2

Chapter One

The Beginning

Bruce Lee was an American from the beginning. He was born in San Francisco's Chinese Hospital Nov. 27, 1940. Though his stay in America would be brief, just two months, he was still an American citizen, a birthright he would one day use to advantage. His mother, Grace Lee, had been left behind in California with friends while her husband, Li Hoi Chuen, continued on to New York City as a prominent member with the traveling company of the Chinese Opera. The San Francisco home where Grace was staying, awaiting the birth of her third child, was, fortuitously, located adjacent to the Chinese Hospital.

The Lee's first child, a boy, had died soon after birth; it was both a terrible loss and an omen. It was felt one of the many Chinese gods had found disfavor with Grace or her husband. The loss of a boy child was, and sometimes still is, considered a much greater disaster than the death of a girl, and they felt compelled to try to confuse the angry spirits. To this end they adopted a baby girl since superstition dictates the second child be a girl. In truth she was not so much adopted as purchased, and for "very small money" it was said. They named the daughter Phoebe. Several months later in Hong Kong, Grace gave birth to a healthy boy, justifying the idea of having deceived

"Bruce was the king gorilla, boss of the whole school."

3

the dark spirits by adopting Phoebe. They named him Peter. Peter had hardly been born before Grace was again pregnant. What if this next child was another boy? Again precautions must be taken to distract the ominous spirits they could feel hovering near. If a dark hand waited for a boy, the child was lost. This led to Bruce having so many names. When Bruce was born he was given a girl's nickname, "Little Phoenix," as a diversionary tactic, and his ears were pierced to further confound the evil ones. He was born in the year of the dragon and the hour of the dragon, between six and eight in the morning.

That morning in the hospital, Grace decided to use the American spelling of Lee, instead of the Chinese Li, naming him Lee Jun Fan, which means "to go back" or "return to." One of the Chinese characters of his name signified San Francisco, all of which implied that his mother thought her son would one day return to America, and more specifically, San Francisco. How accurately she prophesied. (A nurse at the hospital thought the name was still too Chinese and decided to call him Bruce Lee, the name that ultimately appears on his birth certificate.) Later his name was again changed when it was discovered the Chinese characters symbolizing his name were too similar to those of his grandfather. This time he was called Lee Yuen Kam. At an early age he demonstrated the untiring energy that he would always possess and the family called him "never sits still." His brother, Peter, has said when Bruce was still for any length of time the family assumed he was sick. When he began his early career in film he was given yet another name that reflected his birth year, or "Little Dragon," which in Chinese is Li Sui Loong. Even today in Hong Kong, he is often called by that name. Still, he continued to use the name Jun Fan and the transcript of his stay at the University of Washington shows his name to be Bruce Jun Fan Lee. So Bruce began his short life with nearly as

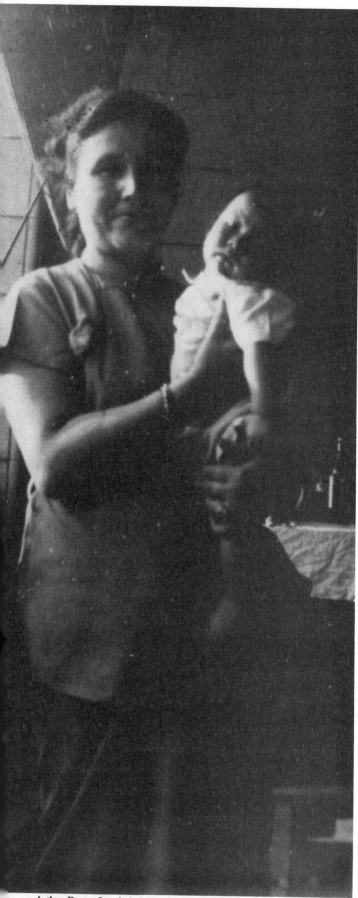

A tiny Bruce Lee is held by his mother, Grace, just months after he was born in a San Francisco hospital. When Bruce was born, he was given a girl's nickname to distract the evil spirits.

Pictured is a touching portrait of Grace Lee and Li Hoi Chuen. Bruce's father was a prominent member with the traveling company of a Chinese opera. While growing up, Bruce and his father had little contact. As such, Bruce grew up on the streets of Hong Kong, a rebellious, unstructured child.

many names as inherited skills. Later a sister, Agnes, would join the growing family, and finally a son, Robert.

Less than a year after the Lees carried their infant son off the boat in Hong Kong, the Japanese military attacked Hong Kong on that infamous date of Dec. 8, 1941. At that same moment, the Japanese were bombing Pearl Harbor in Hawaii, and the rallying cry for Americans became Dec. 7, 1941, one day behind Hong Kong and the international dateline.

He lived on Nathan Road in Kowloon, directly across from a small park where the Japanese occupation headquarters was located. He grew up shaking his fist and shouting at Japanese planes overhead and watching enemy troops dominate the streets and life of Hong Kong. In fact, Bruce's father was nearly killed during the Japanese invasion. He and a friend were sharing an opium pipe when a bomb crashed through the roof and passed Lee only a couple of feet away. Although the bomb never went off, it carried his friend through the floor and to the basement. The man was crushed to death. In Hong Kong alone, approximately 230,000 Chinese died under Japanese rule in less than four years. Bruce heard the many stories of atrocities committed by the soldiers and his hatred hardened toward them. The Chinese had always been subjected to invasion and occupation by one foreign nation or another, more often British, and, probably unknowingly at the time, he wanted to express a pride in being Chinese, but he lacked the means to vent his frustrations. And since the Chinese had lost so many times against invading forces, it was difficult to find something for which to feel proud. This inner conflict surfaced later when he loomed large on a motion picture screen to curse the Japanese. Yet he would also ridicule his fellow countrymen in public for their ancient ways of doing things in what had become a world of modern technology. It was a conflict of love and hate that was held not only by him for the mass of Chinese, but later by these same Chinese for him. He would inflame their pride one moment, then deflate their dreams the next. He even said, publicly, that, "If I'm going to buy a new suit I'd fly to New York before I would have it done here." He said this in the face of 10,000 tailors who ply their trade in Hong Kong. So often he was found torn between America, where he intended to move back at the earliest moment, and his blood ties to China and his countrymen.

Hong Kong came into Britain's possession in 1841 as payment from the Chinese for having defended themselves from these same British forces that had attacked them. It was part of the infamous Opium Wars. Naval Captain Charles Elliot was the man who negotiated the terms of the Chinese surrender wherein the island of Hong Kong was seized as part of the deal. For this Elliot was soundly castigated by the British Foreign Secretary, Lord Palmerson, in London. Palmerson said, "You have disobeyed and neglected your instructions...you have obtained the cession of Hong Kong, a bare island with hardly a house upon it. Now it seems obvious that Hong Kong will not be a mart of trade, anymore than Macao is so."

There was only one reason Hong Kong became useful, and that was for the opium trade. The British plied the Chinese with opium until the nation was nearly destroyed, just as the Japanese plied them with heroin before World War II. So there was a long history of Chinese subjugation under Britain and animosities have been longstanding. The Chinese have, on occasion, tried to rid themselves of the despised British colonial rule and on Jan. 15, 1857, perpetrated what became known as the "Great Poisoned Loaves" plot. As the British citizens sat down to a breakfast that always featured bread or toast, some of the 400 victims noticed an unsavory smell to the bread, all of which had been baked in one particular Chinese bakery. Later that day it was discovered that every loaf of bread had been liberally laced with arsenic; in fact, the bread was excessively laden with poison causing those who ate it to vomit. This excess caused the plot to fail and Britains, in a fury, shrieked for any and all involved in the plot to be summarily hanged. The event finally calmed without a single death being reported, but the colony's British subjects went on strict diets, suspecting all food except that which they could positively verify as free of any possible tampering.

Hong Kong is not, and has never been, a sentimental city. It is sometimes frantically romantic, but never sentimental. Nothing comes in the way of commerical growth. No venerable building or grove of trees will stand once it comes under the eye of business interests. Culturally, Hong Kong is about on par with Calcutta. The excitement of Hong Kong is in its action and its feverish, headlong pursuit of money. Its holidays reflect this preoccupation. At Chinese New Year people raise their voices with "kung hei fat choy," which means "rejoice and grow rich," and another greeting is "kung hei fat fuk," which translates to "Wonderful. You have gained prosperity." Calvin Coolidge would have loved the place.

Bruce's father had prospered as an actor with the Chinese Opera and had purchased several flats that were a source of further income for the family. Still, it was not the family that profited from Lee's ability to make money as much as his cronies in the theater, who could always arrange a "loan," or the gamblers he sported with, or the dealers who supplied him with opium. Lee was a licensed opium smoker and he used it because he said it "helped my theater voice and sweetened my singing." Every theater in Hong Kong had a backstage room to hold a bed and a pipe arrangement for those who needed a quick "tonic." Even now, if screen and stage personalities get together for a benefit show in one of the newer, larger auditoriums, it will have a temporary room constructed backstage for some of the stars to lie down and smoke a bit.

Grace had come to Hong Kong from Shanghai with her Chinese mother and German father at the age of 19. Her father, who was rather well to do, liked to attend the opera and he would often take Grace with him. She became infatuated, as had many a young lady before her, with the show's singer and comic, Lee Hoi Chuen. She would take a position near the orchestra where she "could be seen." It is from such flirtations that empires grow. They were wed and not much later took up residence at 218 Nathan Rd., Kowloon, which would be their home for life, and would, eventually, also house their five children, three servants, and then later, when Lee's brother died, his sister-in-law and her five children. Bruce grew up in these cramped quarters and it was one of the reasons he took to the streets at such an early age. His father had been a casual student of various martial arts styles and had shared some of his training with Bruce. According to Bruce, it was about the only thing his father shared with him. Bruce told many friends that his father, despite his fine income, gave nothing to him. He often spoke of his "miserly" father and would steal from him to take his friends to the cheap restaurants they preferred.

Bruce's film career started in San Francisco during the first two months of his life when he was carried into a scene of a Chinese movie being made in San Francisco, more as a prop than anything else. But the first film in which he had a role was **The Beginning of a Boy** when he was six years old. He never had a featured role until he was 18 and only a short time before he left for the United States. In nearly two dozen films he was indistinguishable from the other

players, but still it was time and experience in front of the camera and it was something of a second life into which he had been born. Later, when he had been cast in American television parts, it was not a unique or unsettling experience. When he walked onto the set to play "Kato" in the "Green Hornet" series, he failed to suffer the trauma normally associated with rookie actors. Van Williams was the actor who played the role of Britt Reid and Bruce often said the only reason he got the part of Kato was because he was the only Chinese in America who could pronounce the name Britt Reid. The average Chinese struggling with English would likely have mispronounced Britt Reid's name as Bwitt Weed.

Bruce enrolled in La Salle College, which is not a college as it is known in the West, but junior and senior high school combined, around 1953 and came under the hand of Brother Henry. A jolly and studious man, Brother Henry is quick to smile a round and pleasant smile, often laughing with a certain joy. He is now in his seventies and retired from teaching, but still living at the school.

During the early 1950s he taught Bruce for a time in a variety of subjects. "He was a very charming boy in many respects," Brother Henry remembers. "Very unique among the many thousands of boys who came through here. He was a bit of a headache to a lot of teachers, but we remained very good friends. Looking back over the years, I am very pleased with the way I dealt with Bruce. I never squashed him or suppressed him. I never believed in teaching with a heavy hand."

Though Brother Henry is a lifelong scholar, and is very precise as a teacher, he recognizes that not all students are like him, nor are they model students. Bruce was very difficult, but Brother Henry realized that Bruce was bright, brighter than many students drawing excellent grades, but he also was a freer "character," and as such

should be dealt with differently. His potential, in many ways, was greater than many straight A students, and it was important that he be nurtured and encouraged for talents that were less observable in the confines of school and compulsory subjects. Brother Henry recognized this, unlike some of the other brothers of La Salle who found him simply unruly, stubborn and lazy. But his interests were not those of his math instructor or biology teacher. Brother Henry lost direct contact with Bruce when he was expelled for poor grades and fighting, but Bruce never forgot Brother Henry, nor did the teacher forget his exceptional charge. Brother Henry says today, "Of all the thousands of boys [he] taught, Bruce stands out the most clearly." And when Bruce would periodically visit Hong Kong, he would always go to La Salle to see his old teacher, finally bringing his family to see the joyous brother.

Brother Henry notes, "I had ways of controlling Bruce and his hyperactive problems. When he would come to school in the morning I would say, 'Bruce, please open all the windows. Please, Bruce would you clean all the blackboards.' He loved to do things and he needed a way to drain some of his phenomenal energy. And I would say, 'Bruce, perhaps you would go to the office and bring the register.'

"Some students say, 'I can do this because my master taught me how to do it.' Bruce might say the same thing, but he would add, 'But I can improve it.'"

When Bruce died, Brother Henry was in Malaysia, a country where Bruce was a great hero and where a high percentage of the population are dedicated gamblers. When the word reached Malaysia that Bruce had died, most couldn't believe it; Bruce was young, robust and a great physical specimen. The gambling establishments immediately posted odds on whether or not he was alive, and the betting began.

Brother Henry told of a scare that Bruce got himself into with the Triads. The Mafialike criminal element in Hong Kong, and most other Chinese communities in the world, is called the Triads, or their more formal name, Three Harmonies Association. It is estimated there are over 100,000 members of this secret society in Hong Kong

alone. They are well financed through extortion rackets, the sale of drugs and control over prostitution. They threaten, coerce, intimidate, terrorize, and sometimes kill to gain their objectives. The Hong Kong film industry is not exempt from their attention. They virtually "own" the supply of "extras" for motion pictures, taking the bulk of these workers' wages as "fees." They also control most of the industry's stuntmen. When Bruce died, one of the rumors concerning his death was that he had been murdered by the Triads for some obscure and ill-defined reason. When a new member is taken into the society he becomes a "blood brother" and swears an allegiance of loyalty which

states, "If I should break my sacred word, may I be hacked to death by 10,000 knives." Their erratic and violent behavior leads to a consuming fear from a chosen victim, as well as his family. They prey on society as do all organizations of this sort, terrorizing the weak, honest, and vulnerable.

During the war, La Salle was under Japanese military occupation, as were nearly all large private and public institutions. Wooden barracks had been constructed on school grounds for students and it was in one of these buildings that Bruce started his school life at La Salle College, though the war had been over nearly six years. The school's staff was housed in a three-story building called The White House. Brother Henry recalls a time when the brothers were having dinner in The White House dining room when a boy rushed in and ran around the table a couple of times and then disappeared into an adjacent telephone room. Brother Richard asked Brother Henry to see what the boy was doing. "So, I went in and found Bruce cowering in one corner of the room, and I told him to get out, but I didn't know he was in danger," recalls Brother Henry. "I found out that he had picked a fight with the son of a Triad chief. You know the Triads? Well, the Triads were after him. He was about 14 at that time, strong and well built. Frisky and strong. The Triads were waiting for him outside on the street and I let him stay awhile before letting him venture out. He went down the staircase, kicking and punching out at the air as he did. I knew that he would not be badly off as the street is public with quite a number of people and there would be La Salle boys around, too. They would help Bruce, because they won't have anyone beating up one of their own like that. Besides, Perth Street is the La Salle boys' territory. They owned Perth Street."

"I have had many successful students in my long career," Brother Henry adds, "but I must admit that I remember Bruce the best. Not for his academic achievements, certainly, but because he was so unique and such a special character. He had self-esteem and great faith in himself."

School only grew in importance to Bruce when he discovered that it was the best, and most reliable way of getting his gang together for an afternoon of mayhem.

Bruce, after an endlessly boring school day, and followed by his excitement-seeking, marauding band of boys, would leave La Salle College and turn down La Salle Road to Prince Edward Road to Boundry and Argyle Streets, hence to Tin Kwong Road, or Dawn Road in its anglicized version. Tin Kwong Road was their final destination,

anticipation growing with every stride. Now they were outside the gate that led to King George V School. This was one of the most fertile places Bruce ever found to engage in trouble.

Here their day was really beginning, with school but a faded, distasteful memory. Here's where life was, where they were going to beat someone up. Either they would meet a group of English boys coming along Tin Kwong Road and the taunting and pushing would begin, or they would have to heap insults onto the boys who were behind the fence on the playing field until tempers overcame common sense. In any case, the fight would finally get underway and Bruce was the catalyst, chopping, punching and kicking his way to schoolboy glory. The English boys were generally bigger, common for boys of European stock, but this was of no concern to Bruce, who found that all the more exhilarating. The theory of "the bigger they come, the harder they fall" was operational. Bruce generally won. Still, in his eyes he "could not" lose. He would not accept being beaten fair and square.

One of Bruce's young fighting friends was Michael Lai, who later became a fine musician and well-known composer of Asian film score. They met on a film set when they were eight years old, having been cast in the same picture and receiving the same salary for the entire production—$125. "We used to stroll along the street, looking for trouble," Michael said. "We had what we call 'Man Chok yee sik,' which is to say we had much national or ethnic pride. Nationalism, as they say. We liked to beat up the English boys."

The British have, for several centuries, been thoroughly hated by the Chinese, in some ways even more than the Japanese. Not only did Bruce work off his aggressions against these boys, but it was sustained by patriotic fervor. He saw it as serving the wishes of his countrymen; not that Bruce needed an excuse for fighting because he often took on the Chinese boys from other gangs as well. When Bruce lost he would blame some other factor for his defeat. Michael Lai recalled "Bruce hated to lose. If he lost, he would have some excuse and never admitted that he had been beaten fairly. He had 'nga tsat,' which is to say he was very cheeky and strutted like a peacock. He always acted very superior."

Their fights would continue until someone, invariably the boys from King George, would yell "quits," or the police arrived.

The Lee home was called by the police on occasion and Peter remembers answering the phone, but saying nothing as the officer at the police station identified himself. He simply kept quiet and finally the officer hung up. Later, a police officer rapped at the door, but Peter, still home alone, did not answer the persistent knocking and the officer finally went away and they heard nothing more.

His father worked in the theater until late at night and when he came home Bruce would either be asleep or hiding under his blanket to avoid being seen. Bruce's mother often protected him from her husband, as he was very strict and observed Chinese customs that dictated a much more obedient and compliant son. Bruce was almost always in rebellion and if he and his father had seen more of one another their lives together under the same roof would probably have been unbearable. As it was, Bruce was getting into more and more trouble and the police began taking note of this "growing sore."

To avoid the intervention of police or passing adults, Bruce's gang would issue challenges to other gangs to meet them on the rooftop of the 12-story Mirador Mansion Building in Tsuishatsui, which is a section of Kowloon. A small elevator grinds to the 12th floor to open on a dingy hallway that turns to allow one boy at a time up a flight of concrete steps and through a door to the roof. It is not a "mansion" as the word is recognized in the West. A two-foot wall surrounds the roof and there are several wide, open spaces allowing room to fight. These spaces are now hemmed by a tangle of television antenna, but there was little television in Hong Kong when Bruce fought there. This is where Bruce honed his "street skills."

Another boyhood friend was Robert Chan, who went with Bruce's sister, Phoebe, for 13 years until they had an argument and decided it was best to go their own ways. Robert tells of Bruce coming home from school holding his hand over one eye and going directly to his room. He had a badly bruised and blackened eye and could not let his father see it because his father had forbidden him to fight. He did not come out of his room at dinner time for two weeks. His mother knew, of course, and she covered for him with a story she concocted, but eventually it became "chun bo," which means the earthen pot was broken and the secret was out. His father was very angry and again restricted Bruce's movements, though his father was not home enough to enforce any edict.

Bruce was 14 and his problems were compounding. His father knew nothing of his street life, nor that Bruce was doing so poorly in school. He did not know of the fights that Bruce was having in a daily fashion, but he agreed with his wife when she came to him with a proposal from their son. Bruce felt a need to learn skills that he could use to "defend" himself from the many ruffians who patrolled the dangerous streets outside their home. He told them he needed expert instruction so he might fend off "bullies" that he met upon leaving school each day. The Lees wondered where there might be such a school and Bruce was ready with that answer, too. He had heard a great deal about a school where a form of kung-fu was taught and whose reputation was unassailable. The school was known to teach a style called wing chun. His parents agreed to stand the cost.

It might be well to digress a moment and reveal something of the background of the

school of martial arts called wing chun, though some of its history may be considered folklore.

A legend persists concerning the birth of the celebrated derivative of kung-fu fighting, wing chun. In about 1720, the Manchu government sent troops to destroy the monastery of Siu Lam in China and kill the Buddhist monks that could be found. Only those who joined the Manchu forces were spared. The Siu Lam monastery was renowned for its training of hand-to-hand combat techniques and the Manchu government wanted it razed before it became a threat. Most of the loyal monks were either killed or burned to death along with the monastery. A few escaped, among them mistress Ng Mui, the only female member of the monastery. This nun went into hiding at the White Crane monastery near a mountain called Tai Leung. Here she meditated and practiced Siu Lam kung-fu, worried that the traitorous monks were equally as skilled in the ways of Siu Lam. She needed a system that would be superior

to Siu Lam. It is said from her window she witnessed a fight between a fox and a crane which featured various striking, parrying and blocking moves one might adapt to the movements of the human body. The attacks and counterattacks of the fox and crane were so skillful and clever that Ng Mui envisioned a new fighting form. She spent many years developing and perfecting this new style.

Meanwhile, another monk, Yim Yee, who had also escaped death at the monastery, had taken his young daughter and settled in a village near Tai Leung mountain. To support them, he sold bean curd from a small stall that was patronized by the Buddhist nun. The years passed and Yim Yee's daughter grew to be a beautiful and graceful young lady, which brought her to the attention of a notorious ruffian who had bullied the villagers into submission. He decided this young woman was to be his wife. His demands came to the attention of mistress Ng Mui, who immediately spirited the girl away to the White Crane monastery, where,

A rare picture of Bruce Lee and the late Yip Man, grandmaster of the modern-day wing chun system. Bruce loved Yip Man and credited him with providing his martial arts foundation. However, when Yip Man died in 1972, Bruce was chastised for not going to his famous teacher's funeral.

for three years she taught the girl the fighting style Ng Mui had perfected. When Ng Mui was satisfied with the girl's training, she sent her back to her father. The thug was soon aware that Yee's daughter had returned and immediately accosted her in the village square. What occurred, of course, became legend. She repulsed the man and sent him away in disgrace using a fighting style never seen before. The girl's name was Yim Wing Tsun, or Wing Chun to the Western ear.

Yim Wing Chun soon married Leung Bok Chau, a boxer of some reputation whom she trained in the art. He passed on the secrets to an herbal physician, Leun Lan Kwai, who in turn passed the skills to a swarthy actor of the Chinese Opera named Wong Wah Bo. The art then was turned over to Leung Yei Tei, who poled barges on the river and added staff techniques to wing chun. Late in life, Leung Yei Tei trained Leung Jan, a respected physician of Chopsticks Street in Fatshan. Leung Jan became so famous as a fighter that he was called "kung-fu king" of wing chun. Many years passed before Leung Jan found anyone he

could trust with the skills—his own sons, Leung Tsun and Leung Bik. Others came along, continuing the line of succession, such as Wah the Wooden Man, and Chan Wha Shun, the moneychanger. Wah the money-changer was over 70 when he found his 16th and last disciple. This young man was 13 at the time he began his training under the moneychanger, continuing until the old man died. Although this young man did not begin to teach until he was 56, he became the most illustrious sifu of them all—Yip Man. Nearly 300 years after the nun, Ng Mui, initiated the system, Yip Man taught his most famous student, Bruce Lee. When Yip Man introduced wing chun training to Bruce, he was completely absorbed. Yip Man said Bruce became "fighting crazy." The equivalent in America are the thousands of inner city school boys who can be seen dribbling a basketball wherever they go, on the way to school, boarding a bus, or in the subway. Or even sitting at a table. They live basketball the way Bruce lived his kung-fu training. He embraced his new training with a fanatical zeal that would last his lifetime. Interestingly,

17

Yip Man, at a younger age, also sought out English boys to test his skills and sharpen his techniques.

Bruce was a sickly baby and there was nothing about him to suggest he would, one day, be the epitome of the male physique. His finely tuned body was the product of great effort and unstinting work. He trained, starting about his 20th birthday, without pause to the end of his life. Later, as a star living in Kowloon Tong, he was often seen stopping his Mercedes in the driveway of his home and starting for the door that led to his exercise machine. He would take off his jacket and shirt as he went, hardly stopping for a hello before beginning the afternoon's training. He was a demanding perfectionist who asked more from himself than he ever asked of others.

Bruce's urge for combat began at an early age. His friend, Robert Chan, tells of using the family car and the Lee chauffeur to go to a place called To Fong Shan, where they could catch "kam see mau," which literally means "golden-haired cat," though it was not a cat but a kind of large dark beetle that has a fringe of golden hair. They would place the beetles in the trough of a length of bamboo, and goad them into fighting. Bruce seemed to enjoy any form of combat and was drawn to its excitement and challenge.

In those days tens of thousands of Chinese were fleeing the unfathomable Communist regime on the Mainland and Hong Kong was being overwhelmed by refugees pouring into the colony. There was nowhere near enough available housing to handle this daily horde. They took up residence on the streets in cardboard lean-tos, in doorways, and on the unpredictable hillsides that often took them sliding into the gullies during the heavy rains. Many died trying to live. They became squatters on building tops, resisting every effort by the authorities to dislodge them. When the hot summer weather dried out the city, fire was a continual threat. Bruce saw much of this as daily routine, and at Christmastime in 1953, the year he joined Yip Man's school, a fire raged through squatters shanties in Kowloon just a couple miles from his home on Nathan Road. The disaster left 50,000 people homeless. Aware of the plight of his fellow Chinese and how they always seemed plagued by the forces of nature and man, he would always defend their position when facing the world.

Bruce had little regard for formal education and did not do well in studies other than art and history. His mother said he was ten years old before he could count to ten. His inability to sit quietly and listen caused many an interruption in class and he was in conflict with teachers and supervisors from the outset. This led to several expulsions. As soon as he was old enough to challenge another boy on the street, he did so. No matter what expression a boy might assume, Bruce found it to be an affront. If the boy smiled it was surely a smirk, and if the boy frowned it demonstrated a surly attitude. Bruce could find reason to fight from the way a boy stood, slouched or combed his hair. When Bruce was out on the street looking for a fight, he found fault in the way a boy said hello, and **no one** could stare him down. "He could stare holes in rocks!" it was said. Bruce had a natural inclination toward aggressive behavior. His temperament was such that he had to learn how to fight or be killed. He was a "small and skinny kid," who pugnaciously stood his ground against everyone. He believed he could win the world by beating it into submission.

Every year La Salle College held an open boxing tournament. One boy, a European, had been boxing champion for several years, prior to Bruce being enrolled in La Salle. Though Bruce was younger and considerably smaller, he defeated the champion with relative ease. He told his friend Robert Chan that he did not throw a punch for some time, content with blocking the heavier boy's

punches and warding off the blows until the European's strength had waned. Then he rushed in with a flurry of quick punches that buried his foe. He immediately became a hero of the undergraduates and now they were willing to do his homework **without** his threatening them. Robert Lee said his brother "was the king gorilla, boss of the whole school."

Robert, eight years younger than Bruce, was a source of some worry because Bruce saw him starting off and out onto the streets as Bruce had done, a feisty, impish boy. Bruce felt he needed advice and guidance, something of which Bruce had gotten little. Bruce called him "gav-jai," which means "little dog or dog boy." Robert idolized his brother and would have, if allowed, helped fight Bruce's fight and run the streets. He recalls eating off the street with Bruce, gobbling up orange-colored chicken claws, pig intestines, sea urchins and the like, both taking it in like an American boy with his chocolate bars. Later Bruce paid Robert's passage to the United States as well as his school tuition and maintenance. He did not want Robert to follow his example and run wild in the streets.

During his teen years, Bruce was much the ladies man. He was good looking, a great dancer and dressed in the mode of the day. His brothers speak of the many hours Bruce stood before mirrors, combing his hair, using the hair dryer and preening. Every hair had its place and learned to find it. When he took to his favorite place, the street, he was ready for any encounter, from a new girl to an old fight, a steel chain wrapped around his waist and hidden under his jacket.

One of these new girls was a pretty teen-ager by the name of Amy Chan, who would later become known in Asia by her film name, Pak Yan. They seldom had enough money to pay for entertainment and they would often go down by the railroad station where, using long bamboo poles, they would knock flowers from the magnolia and loquat trees to make bouquets. It was an innocent time for Bruce and Pak, a more quiet moment at the outset.

"He was a very good person with many high principles. A very nice man, a very good friend," Pak remembers. "He helped his friends, that is to say, when a friend needed help you could be sure he would be there. Within his power he would do anything for a friend."

Surrounded by the other members of his gang, they walked the streets these nights and when they got hungry Bruce would stop at the Nathan Road flat to take any money he could find. Then it was off to a "big meal" and a "tea dance."

Bruce usually lacked enough money to go to nightclubs, but many establishments set aside two hours on weekend afternoons to hold "tea dances." During these hours the prices were much reduced, akin to "happy hour" in many Western bars, and the band and singers would arrive early. The place Bruce would frequent, and has since been torn down, was the Bay Side Night Club in Tsimshatsui. During the tea dance, Bruce would dance his head off for the allotted time.

Pak had met Bruce's parents and re-members Grace being quite "Westernized" and open minded, but Lee Sui Loong was "very antique," which is to say conservative.

Pak says of Bruce, "When he played, he played like mad." Pak said being around Bruce was never dull. You were either laughing uncontrollably, or shouting at him in anger. When she was alone with him he was quiet, but if they were joined by others he was very chauvinistic. Whatever he said **must** be done. Pak's father was in the film industry and arranged for Pak to test for a part at the National Film Studio, a film company that no longer exists. She got a small part that required her to cha-cha, which she had never learned. She asked Bruce, who had been crowned cha-cha champion of Hong Kong not long before, if

he would teach her. Of course he would. This was only a few months before he left for the United States and Pak Yan did not see him for five years until he came back in 1964, the year he married Linda Emery in Seattle. Pak Yan, in those five years, had become a famous star in Asia and was being featured in one film after the other. When she heard that Bruce was in Hong Kong she phoned him and told him that she had been cast in a film called **San San**. She explained the character in the story was "a bad girl." Would Bruce teach her how to be "a bad girl?" Of course he would, and did for several weeks.

He told Pak, in 1959, that he was going to the United States and open a "mo-kun," or martial arts school, but that he would never teach the "gwie-los," or "foreign devils" any of the secrets of Chinese fighting techniques. He feared they would then bully the Chinese. As it turned out, he was the first to teach the "gwie-los" these same secrets.

Fourteen years later, Bruce would be dead and his funeral would be held in the Kowloon Funeral Parlor on Maple Street. Pak Yan, now famous, would want to attend the funeral to offer her condolences, but she could not. She knew the press reporters would be hovering close by and looking for any sign of emotion from the women in attendance. "I would have cried," she said, "and the reporters would see that and they would want to know why Pak Yan cries. I was married by then and I have children. They would trace back and they would make a big story out of our knowing each other. I didn't want to go through that, or have my family involved. So I stayed home and cried. I still remember July 20. July 20."

Frequently a young man by the name of Siu Kee Lun, or better known in Hong Kong as Unicorn, would join Pak Yan and Bruce. In many ways he was closer to Bruce than any of the other boys, which made his betrayal of Bruce years later all the more disappointing. Unicorn was much like Bruce's slave, running errands, seeing to Bruce's needs and idolizing him. His career, for some time, ran parallel to Bruce's, getting small parts in films and working as a stuntman. This could have been Bruce's life had he not left Hong Kong for the United States and broken a pattern long followed by would-be Chinese actors. Left behind, Unicorn decided he was in no way inferior to Bruce. People in Hong Kong tell of the bitterness which grew with Bruce's successes in America and how Unicorn felt he had been denied the chance to bloom in his own right.

One of the rooftop encounters, which was supposed to be a simple sparring match between the leaders of two schools, turned into a serious fight when Bruce was bopped in the eye with an unexpected punch. Bruce stared at the young man for a few moments— a stare that would become world famous— and the boys from both schools backed away. Bruce went on the attack with a landslide of punches to drive the boy back across the white line that had been painted on the roof as a way to declare the winner. But Bruce's temper was soaring and he followed across the line to kick the boy in the face a few times and knock out a couple teeth.

When the parents of the boy saw his damaged face, they went straight to the police and lodged a complaint against Bruce. Grace Lee was obliged to appear at the police station and accept responsibility for her son's behavior and was then required to sign a form stating she would "see" about Bruce and that they would both be accountable if any further reports were received of Bruce fighting "this woman's son." Mrs. Lee's son could well find himself in jail.

Again, Bruce's father was not informed that his son was in trouble. After having been expelled from La Salle College, Bruce was being threatened with removal from Saint Francis Xavier High School, where he had gone following his life at La Salle. His impending dismissal stemmed from familiar causes—poor attitude and subpar grades.

Chapter Two

America

Mrs. Lee sat down with her belligerent and beleaguered son. She had already heard from her son Peter, who told her that Bruce had made some serious enemies who had sworn to kill him. "Some of his friends," Peter said, "and some of his enemies were Triads, though Bruce, himself, had never joined the organization." Grace had to do something. She and Bruce agreed that he had to leave Hong Kong, and since he was an American citizen, there would be no difficulty with the immigration people. The two told Bruce's father that he was going to seek his fortune in the United States and his father gave the move his blessing. There might have even been a sigh of relief from the old comic. Bruce promised to "make something of myself." Grace folded a $100 bill in his hand, and in October, 1958, he sailed for San Francisco on the American Presidents Line.

It was 1958 and Bruce returned to the city of his birth. He was in the country where he had promised himself that he would show his father he could make good. He started out slowly, beginning with what he knew best—dancing. That he was a gifted ballroom dancer is unchallengeable, and he began giving cha-cha lessons, something he also did aboard ship on his way to San Francisco. During a break at a dance in San Francisco, Bruce gave an exhibition of his wing chun

"You look like
you can fight."

training. The demonstration was witnessed by a young man who passed on what he had seen to his brother, acknowledged kung-fu expert James Lee. Lee showed an interest in this new import from Hong Kong, but did not follow up on the information. Only later would James Lee play a large part in Bruce's life.

During Bruce's short stay in San Francisco he was joined by his brother, Peter, who would travel with Bruce to Seattle for a brief time before traveling east to the University of Wisconsin. He eventually became a scientist of some repute, and is now second in command of Hong Kong's Royal Observatory.

Peter said, "We slept together in an old double bed. Every once in a while Bruce would be taken with a dream and start punching out and yelling, and once, literally tore his pajamas apart as he punched and kicked out in a violent demonstration. Then he'd start kicking and throwing the covers off us before settling back for the rest of the night. He was tight and tense even in his sleep." His commitment to his training was self-consuming even then. He gave very little thought to any other subject, other than philosophical readings that he could relate to the martial arts.

The start of Bruce's American career was short-lived as a problem grew around him in San Francisco that has never been satisfactorily explained. Personality flaws dogged Bruce his entire life, heightened by his quick temper and his inability to cope with real and imagined affronts, no matter how slight. So much of the time he dealt with the world in a state of defiance. His mother was obliged to call family friends in Seattle, Ping and Ruby Chow, and arrange for Ruby to take the rebellious 18-year-old and shelter him in her restaurant. Grace told Ruby she would send some money to help with his upkeep, and it was agreed that no one would tell his father about this arrangement. It was Bruce's impression that he was to go to school in Seattle and act as "uncle" to Ruby's youngest son, Mark. Ruby put him in a tiny, third-floor bedroom and promptly set him to work in the kitchen as a busboy. There was an instant clash of wills and the growth of an animosity that was never to be resolved or softened. To Ruby Chow, Bruce was just another of many young men who floated in from Hong Kong, and would probably soon float out just as quickly.

Ruby does not like to talk about those days with Bruce because she won't say anything about anyone unless she can say something good. This leads her to talk very little about Bruce. Ruby told her brood, "He's here and it's no problem. I'll put him to work and he'll have a little spending money." Ruby's place was virtually a boarding house and a funnel for dozens of Chinese coming from China and Hong Kong. In retrospect it would appear that, despite all their fights, Ruby molded Bruce into something more than he had been. There is no doubt that Ruby was a rough awakening for this wild truant, and though he probably never admitted it, she was one of the more important reasons for his going forward in a more serious and responsible manner. Ruby Chow gave structure and discipline to Bruce's life, even though he resisted and fought all the way. It was something he badly needed, though he was quite unaware of it at the time.

The link between the Lee and Chow families went back many years and was the reason Bruce found himself in Seattle. Ruby's aunts and uncles were poor when they arrived in Seattle. Ruby was born and raised in Seattle, quite poor but strong and tough. She had to lift herself and her family out of the Chinese ghetto. Ruby showed her strength early on when she divorced her first husband. Divorce was frowned upon by

Bruce's skills as a dancer were known throughout Hong Kong, where he was crowned cha-cha champion. He even earned money as a dance teacher during his voyage from Hong Kong to America.

Chinese in those days and for a wife to divorce her husband was a very singular thing. Husbands might, on occasion, divorce their wives, and husbands might play around and leave or abandon their wives, but wives did not divorce husbands. Rudy did. Ruby was single and bright and ambitious. She wanted to make a mark in the world and, in those times, New York City was the only place to go. Soon after her arrival in New York City she met an actor from Hong Kong, who, **fortunately**, was sick. Deserted by his girl friends, Ruby nursed him back to health. The actor's name was Ping Chow, who was a member of Hong Kong's Cantonese Opera that had been stranded in the U.S. with the outbreak of war with the Japanese on December 7, 1941. The Cantonese Opera had a small circle of players who learned to take care of one another. They drew together in a fraternal manner, becoming virtual brothers. Ping Chow and Bruce's father were such a pair. Soon Ruby and her new husband were back in Seattle and later still, in 1955, they decided to start a Chinese restaurant,

outside Chinatown. No Chinese had ever attempted such a thing and many thought they were crazy. They chose a large three-story home at Broadway and Jefferson which had been a hotel with an Italian restaurant on the first floor. Ruby's restaurant prospered and finally became a Seattle landmark before being torn down in 1985 to make way for a medical building.

Ruby was one of the most powerful people in Seattle and the most influential Chinese in the city for many years. When Chinese had problems with the city, its police, the immigration people, or had social and financial difficulties, they went to Ruby. She was the quintessential community spokesman. She was universally respected in city government, and later was elected county commissioner. From that lofty position, she trumpeted the cause of her people in city hall and the courts. Staff in Seattle hospitals called her to translate for patients who could not speak English, and the police would come to her to arbitrate problems on a neighborhood street level. She was proud of

being Chinese, which was one of the few areas where she and Bruce agreed. Ruby would say, "The Chinese are the best. Nobody is better than the Chinese. They are superior." She had a reputation of hating the Japanese, but she says that was untrue. Ruby's denial tends to ring true since three of her sons married Japanese girls.

She was the world's first woman member of the Chong Wah Benevolent Association and the first woman president of a chapter of the Chong Wah. The Chong Wah Association was formed to serve Chinese who found themselves away from mother China and who did not belong to a Tong (local family association.) The Republic of China in Taipei invited her and Ping to attend its worldwide conclave. The first time she went she caused some trauma among the all-male membership. They had known that an American woman had been elected to the post, but having her there caused some grumbling. In fact, no one at the convention would talk to her or Ping, and it was only on the last day of the convention that they discovered that everyone thought Ping was Ruby's gigolo (possibly because Ping still looked so young.) Even today, though both she and Ping are retired, people come to her with their problems. They arrive from Taiwan and Hong Kong, where they have been told to find Ruby when they get to America and that she will take care of their needs. "My mom is my mom," is the way Ruby's youngest son, Mark, puts it. Meaning for all her faults and attributes, she is what she is and she's not about to change. "My father and mother could be rich now if they hadn't given money to so many and helped so many," Mark says. "That's the way they are and they don't feel bad for not being rich." They took in people without a thought and housed many a basketball team and other groups, feeding and finding places for them to sleep. As many as 30 at a time.

This is the woman under whose rules and disciplines Bruce had fallen. It was a smoking standoff for the couple of years Bruce spent there, but he was not the worst for the experience. When Bruce lived and worked in Ruby Chow's he had a room "no bigger than a closet." It was another reason he hated his life there. He had come from a rather well-to-do family in Hong Kong and now he was "less than a busboy" and treated in a like manner. He was used to being pampered. Top man. Here he was low man on a greased pole. He didn't like the way Ruby treated him, and, conversely, Ruby didn't like the way he treated her. She would say, "Bruce, you call me Auntie Ruby." Bruce would not do it. He would say, "You're no Auntie of mine." And many times there would be a shouting match. Ruby expected the respect due her, which is understood even more clearly in the Chinese culture, but Bruce would not succumb. He never deferred to anyone. Ever.

So they would go at one another tooth and nail. Grace was sending money to Bruce without her husband's permission even when Bruce was working at Ruby's. Bruce was getting peanuts for the menial chores he performed and sometimes his gang stood around behind the restaurant, waiting for him to finish his work before they could get a training session underway. Other times Bruce would have to break off in the middle of a session to get back to his job at the restaurant. He felt Ruby was taking advantge of him. He believed he had been sent to Seattle to go to school and be Ruby's house guest. No one had ever given Bruce a work schedule; Ruby was the first to ever really knock him down. She was an unassailable wall. It was during this period that Bruce went from street punk to someone bent on making something of himself.

Soon after his arrival in Seattle he met a group of young toughs who were members of several street gangs that permeated the city

Bruce did just about everything he could, including teaching dance, to escape from the clutches of Ruby Chow and her restaurant. He never saw eye to eye with Ruby, who considered him just another one of the boys.

in the 1950s. Edison Vocational School, where Bruce was a student, had set aside a day to honor its Asian students and to show various aspects of Asian culture and activity. All of Seattle was taken up with what they called Asian Day. Bruce had been asked to perform a few martial arts techniques and some of the streetfighters had seen a notice of this tacked to a bulletin board. They decided to take in "this nonsense." One of the toughs was a bright and articulate, but burly and rough-looking young man named James DeMile, who even today looks like a man one would not want to enrage. Seattle's gangs were often named after hills of the city. Jim DeMile was the leader of the Capitol Hill mob.

Bruce would insist that the gang surround him as bodyguards when they would "run" the streets. People would have to give way to this advancing menace, wondering who the snappily dressed, handsome Chinese was among them. If someone asked, he was told that Bruce was the rich son of the Chinese ambassador.

Writer Jim Halpin interviewed DeMile for an article in *Inside Kung-Fu* magazine and this is his account of the first meeting:

"Bruce arrived all dressed up in a dark suit and tie," DeMile recalled. "He was so neatly turned out that all he needed was a black book under his arm to make him look like a Mormon missionary. The suit hid his physique so what you saw was this frail-looking, 18-year-old kid wearing thick, round spectacles. On top of that, he had this weird Hong Kong accent and speech impediment that made his r's sound like w's. Bruce looked about as dangerous as Don Knotts; if somebody had told me I'd spend the next two years watching him transform himself into the most lethal human fighting machine in the world, I would have thought he was hallucinating."

Lee told his audience that they had never heard of gung-fu, which Bruce spelled in the Cantonese manner, because it was not available to Westerners. The Chinese kept gung-fu secret, Bruce said, so it could never be used against them in a fight. At no time, DeMile recalled, did Lee ever hint that his art was popular among the punks and thugs of Hong Kong. At first, Bruce cleverly hid his style by demonstrating fighting movements named and patterned after animals. Bruce first assumed the eagle stance with his hand extended in a claw, then transformed himself into a praying mantis with his forearms making piano-hammer strikes. Then he was a white crane with its wings spread and its leg raised in the defense position.

"It was a beautiful performance," DeMile said, "sort of a cross between ballet and mime, but it sure didn't look like fighting and the audience began to titter."

Bruce suddenly became still, "Like a cat who's just seen a robin," DeMile said. "The audience got very quiet very quickly, too, and I got my first intimation this guy might really not be all talk. He got some sucker to come up front and suddenly he's all over this guy. He starts explaining how he would tear this guy apart like an overcooked chicken and mimes how he'd cave in his temples with a praying mantis strike, then rip his muscles apart, rip out his windpipe and tear his rib cage asunder. It was vivid and nobody was laughing anymore, but I had my doubts and they must have showed because next thing I know, Bruce is looking right at me saying, "You look like you can fight, how about coming up here for a minute?"

DeMile, who then was 20 years old and 220 pounds of gristle, could indeed fight. He was a former undefeated heavyweight champion of the Air Force, as well as an unscarred veteran of a hundred streetfights. Never having lost a fight, DeMile was unimpressed by the challenge. "None of my fights had

When Bruce Lee first demonstrated his talents at an Asian exhibition, Seattle's young toughs couldn't believe this smallish, handsome Chinese kid could fight. They discovered differently, however, when he challenged them to hit him.

ever lasted more than a second or two," DeMile said, "partly because I was as unsqueamish as a hog butcher about shedding blood. And it didn't matter how many of them I was up against. If it was a gang, I'd just pick out the leader, break his leg, and the rest of them would usually run off while he was screaming around on the ground." Any apprehension DeMile might have harbored was, in any case, eliminated when Lee said he would use wing chun, a little-known system devised by an ancient Buddhist nun. Bruce turned to DeMile and invited him to hit as hard as he could with either hand.

"I couldn't believe this guy," DeMile recalled. "It's easy to block a fast punch if you know which hand is coming first, but if you don't know it's quite another matter. Anyway, I fired a straight right hoping it wouldn't take his head off in front of 40 witnesses. I needn't have worried. He blocked me easily and gave me a left that stopped just short of my nose. From then on, no matter what I did, he tied me up with "sticky hands" and punched back at will, always stopping the blow in the last possible millimeter. I can't tell you how devasting this was. My identity was founded on never having lost a fight and here I was all tied up and helpless. I felt like I was in a slow-motion nightmare. And it didn't help things when Bruce unmercifully ended it all by knocking me on my forehead with a knuckle and asking if anyone was home. I knew I had to either find out what this guy knew or go into intensive therapy, so after the demonstration I swallowed what little was left of my pride and asked him if he'd teach me some of his techniques."

Bruce began to work these young men, who, in many ways, were not so different from him. They all had kinship of the street and the brotherhood of that life. DeMile said, "I was an inept kid in his hands. Even to this day, when I think back, I'm amazed at what he could do to us. It was effortless and it was great, especially, if it was happening to somebody else. So we were drawn to him. Each of us got something different from him and for different reasons. Some were less interested in the fighting than the philosophy Bruce bandied about."

This "gang" of Bruce's ran together from 1959—1963. He was not the mythical giant of movie fame that he was to become, but a mere mortal struggling to better himself in a parking lot behind Ruby Chow's place. This was another significant "passage" for Bruce because he learned as much as he taught, using these willing victims as "studies." Later he pulled himself free of these gritty beginnings and went off in search of immortality.

DeMile claims he developed the famous one-inch punch along with Bruce, the punch that Bruce incorporated into the wing chun system. It is a matter of snapping the wrist when applying power at a distance very close to the opponent. It was, and is, devastating, and can be lethal. DeMile still demonstrates the punch at seminars and says no one else can do it, including Danny Inosanto, who later became Bruce's protege'. DeMile says neither Bruce nor he ever taught it to anyone.

This gang was very close, eating together, going to movies together, training together.

At about this time, because of a severe eye affliction, Bruce began wearing contact lenses. Luckily, a member of his group had a job with a company that made them and he got them for little money. However, he was always losing them. He lost one at a demonstration in Chinatown during Chinese New Year, DeMile remembers. Bruce stopped the performance and began searching between the floorboards of the stage, enlisting everyone's help until they literally tore the stage apart.

Long before he created the style known as jeet kune do, Bruce Lee's martial arts foundation was based on the Chinese style of wing chun.

He and his small company of soldiers would sometimes go into a restaurant, moving slowly around the tables because Bruce would be staring straight ahead through the milk-white eyes of a new pair of contact lenses. Bruce would feel for an empty chair, possibly at a table already occupied, but the gang would lead him to a suitable table. He would sit and stare vacantly across the table, faking blindness. Nonetheless, he would ask the waiter for a menu and the waiter, rather skeptically, would place it on the table in front of him. Bruce would feel and finger the menu, finding the edge to open it. Then, staring vacuously across the table, he would pass his hand over the menu, hovering a couple inches above it. By now the waiter would be staring wide-eyed and Bruce would begin to order his dinner in Chinese. The gang would interpret for the waiter. The waiter would be a little shaken, perceiving this to be a demonstration of supernatural powers from the mysterious Far East. The gang would explain that Bruce had what amounted to a third eye, but not to worry.

Other times Bruce would wear lenses that glowed bright red. He would step up to a theater ticket booth, his head bowed and his eyes unseen, to ask for a ticket. He would hand over a bill, not once looking at the girl in the booth. She would slip the ticket and his change under the glass partition and then Bruce would slowly lift his head to stare at her, grinning. Some were known to have screamed. These were his "dragon eyes."

Bruce was not a good waiter. He was not meant to wait on people and did not have the proper attitude. "When you're serving people, you're **serving** people," Mark Chow

said. "My mother insisted on perfect service." It had to be done one way and her standards were rigid. A waiter was to be polite and there was never to be an empty teacup or a cold teapot. The water glass was to be lifted off and away from the table, filled and returned to the table. Bruce did not care for this regimentation. He did not easily take orders and there were numerous complaints about his attitude. But Ruby had her rules of behavior and these two were in constant confrontation about the structure of the restaurant and how things were to be done. Bruce was never subservient to anyone and his entire bearing set itself contrary to the role a waiter must assume. Being a waiter was possibly the worst job Bruce could be asked to do and it led to many a dissatisfied or aggravated customer. Bruce was often a disruptive force in the restaurant. There are accounts of problems between he and the other employees, and even of a cook angrily chasing him with a meat cleaver until the cook was restrained by his helpers.

There are thousands of people in this world who claim to have been taught **by** Bruce Lee, and thousands more who claim to have **taught** Bruce Lee. Of these thousands there were no more than 50 who actually came under his tutelage, and only **two** of these can say that he had been a friend. And of these two, neither can truthfully say that Bruce was completely known to them. Linda Emery, who was to become his wife, said, "Bruce and the Lee family have secrets." Beyond Linda, only one person can be believed to be a certain friend. His name is Taky Kimura and he's lived in Seattle most of his life. His story and his relationship to Bruce are important.

Chapter Three

Taky

Taky was born in 1924 and brought up in the small Washington town of Clallam Bay on the Olympic peninsula. It was a railroad and lumber town and Taky's father was a foreman to a gang of Japanese laborers. Men such as these were called "gandy dancers" for reasons that Taky cannot imagine, and they were employed by the railroad, repairing roadbeds and rails.

Taky worked with such a gang for a summer and "it about killed me." The work was hard and his father "sweated" to raise his family of three girls and three boys. "But there was a certain beauty to it," Taky says. "People helped each other and there was a great respect and feeling for one another." Taky went to the same small school for all of his 12 grades and was set to graduate the June following the Japanese bombing of Pearl Harbor. Taky and his family were served notice that the government saw them to be potentially dangerous Japanese and enemy aliens and that they were to be taken to an internment camp for the duration of the war. The townspeople vouched for the Kimuras and asked that they be allowed to stay, but the government denied the request. His family packed, and on the evening of what would have been graduation, was herded along with other Japanese families onto a truck bound for Port Townsend.

"We were ripe meat for Bruce."

Boarding a train whose windows had been blacked out, they were taken to a camp outside a barren little California town called Lake Toule. The camp was situated in what had been a bird refuge, though it was dry and desertlike when they arrived. Wire fences had been erected and tar paper shacks were being built. The camp eventually held more than 10,000 Japanese-Americans. They grew potatoes and established the acknowledged longest potato row in the world. They formed their own fire department and internal security organization. Taky made $16 a month working in the camp. Professionals such as doctors and dentists received $19 a month. But even at this rate the family put away a small nest egg. The American labor force had dwindled as more and more young men were drafted and recruiters would come into the camp looking for men to work the nearby fields. Rumors, however, had it that "so and so" had gone with men such as these and had been shot in the fields. Taky's parents would not allow him to sign up. Taky spent four-and-a-half years in the camp and was 22 when the war ended and the family was released. But they had no place to go. Taky's older brother was sent to Seattle, but he discovered no one would rent to a Japanese. After weeks of hunting, he finally found a vacant, one-bedroom house at the rear of a home owned by an elderly German.

The landlord agreed to rent the small house until he found out there were eight members to the Kimura family. He couldn't believe that many people could live in such a small house but the brother, with great tenacity, parked on the old man's porch until he reluctantly agreed to have them. Later, when he saw how industrious and neat they were, he added a bedroom to the small building. Now Taky had to find a job, which took months. When he went into a restaurant he would be ignored by everyone, including the waitresses, causing him to leave hungry. It got to the point where, if Taky saw a white person approaching him, he would stop and let the person pass. He had very little self-worth and self-esteem. "I told myself one day," he said, "that I had to do something. I started reading and self-educating and searching. Then I met the girl that was to be my wife, Peggy, who is Caucasian. When she'd put her arm around me in public I'd say, 'Don't do that, Peggy. We could get into trouble.' Interracial couples were very much opposed at that time." Taky refused to waste his energies in hatred, nor did he look backward. He was determined to keep his eye on the goals he had set for himself. He worked as a gardener with another Japanese for a year, then secured jobs in a venetian blind factory and a foundry. The family of three sisters and three brothers considered pooling their efforts and building something together. They had a chance to take over a small hotel in the skid row section of Seattle, but they could not accept all the fighting they saw among the street drunks. Then they found a small grocery store, though grocery people warned them away because it had never been successful. Ignoring the advice, they borrowed money from friends and went into business even though, "We didn't know the price of a quart of milk." When they started doing well the landlady sued them for more money because her friends told her the Kimuras were getting off cheap. She lost in court, but it soured the Kimuras on the location and they started looking again. They found a vacant lot and got a long-term lease to build a store. Now Taky has two supermarkets and is quite well-to-do.

Taky relates, "I had been fooling around with the martial arts a bit and I even took judo training from a Japanese instructor while in the internment camp. Some of the streetfighters, like Jim DeMile, knew I was interested in all that and they'd hang out at the back of the store and we'd work out once in awhile. One day they told me about a kid down in Chinatown who was incredible and that I had to go see him. Well, I'd seen a lot of martial artists, here and in Japan, who were very good and older and more experienced than this kid they were talking about and I couldn't see how he could be any better. But I finally went down there to see for myself. He was giving an exhibition on a baseball field in Chinatown and it was unbelievable. I joined right up." Taky was 38 and Bruce was 18. Jim DeMile says, "Taky was twice our ages and he was more interested in what Bruce had to talk about than what he did. He could sit for long periods and listen to Bruce and the two of them developed a close kinship."

Bruce loved children and often carried a pocketful of wrapped Chinese candy that he would give out to the kids he met. Still, if taxed, his patience would wear out in dealing with people of any age. Bruce had been put in charge of Ruby's youngest son, Mark, who now is an attorney for the mayor of Seattle. Mark, at that time, was about seven years old, and at this particular moment was taking a bath under Bruce's supervision. Mark admits to "wising off and taunting" Bruce in some way. Bruce took this for some time, then suddenly grabbed Mark by the hair and shoved his head under the soapy water. He held him there until Mark was taking in water and struggling for his life. Mark says, "I wasn't alarmed for a few seconds, but after a bit I realized I was **breathing** the water. Then I began to panic. I never told my mother because that would have just caused another huge fight." Mark never again gave Bruce trouble.

Ruby Chow's restaurant was known to be haunted. There was the case of a cook who saw a ghost in the basement and came flying up to leave his employer that day. Ruby claims to have seen a ghost that appeared as a black shadow and pinned her down on the floor on her stomach. She never again slept on her stomach. This same shadow grappled with Bruce as well. He told of being held down for several minutes, drenched in sweat by the time he was finally released. This was probably one of the few times Bruce had been physically defeated. There were other ghostly appearances in the restaurant, but none proved threatening. One cousin who worked for Ruby during those years was jostled as she was taking a tray of dirty dishes to the kitchen. A half-filled teapot tipped over on it side and its contents formed a perfect question mark on the floor. Scoff at your own risk.

Bruce could not help himself from causing mayhem. There was a day at Ruby Chow's when he got the Chow children to play a joke on their young cousin, Rick. They enticed him into a second-floor bedroom and locked the door. He was quite angry and started to pound on the door when out of the closet behind him came Bruce wearing the costume of a grotesque madman. Bruce shrieked and screamed and chased Rick around the room. Frightened to near death, he has never forgiven Bruce or the rest of the children.

In 1959, Bruce began dating a Japanese girl named Amy Sanbo who had also been interred during World War II. Until he met Linda, this was the most serious love affair of his life, and spanned nearly three years. He repeatedly asked her to marry him.

Amy could hardly remember her internment, but she did observe the mistreatment her mother went through because she had refused to sign a loyalty oath as a matter of principle. Then her mother refused to speak anything but Japanese the rest of her life. Bruce would go to Amy's home in Seattle and talk with her mother, using the little Japanese he knew. He got along extremely well with Amy's mother, but not so with Amy.

Jim DeMile remembers Amy saying to Bruce, "Hey, your whole thing is Bruce Lee. All your thoughts, all your dreams, all your goals are Bruce Lee. I haven't heard anything about Amy." And Bruce would answer, DeMile says, with what Bruce saw to be the final argument. "But my goals are so big and so exciting that I want to share them with you." Bruce believed his life was going to be so successful and meaningful that Amy would be happy and content to live a part of it. As many times as Bruce asked her to get married, Amy rejected him, though she admitted that this was not entirely an easy answer. She also felt if a person did well it should be shared with people who had less. She had a pronounced sensitivity to social problems, something that Bruce never considered. His level of consciousness about these people was quite low. He said it was their business. If they wanted to get out of a hole, they would get out. Amy felt that Bruce was immature and shallow and that he only did things for effect. She believed he spouted a great deal of Oriental wisdom that he did not follow himself. This, of course, was Bruce's punk period; a punk kid who had been in trouble in Hong Kong and was well on his way to trouble in Seattle. She saw him as an immature kid with a unique talent. But what then? She wondered why, with Bruce having so much, he had to be such an exhibitionist? He told her he simply wanted to see how people would react to these displays. He felt it was fun and funny. Amy did not find it amusing. The young men around Bruce only saw a knowledge they felt was profound, and an expert in the martial arts. What Amy saw and what the gang saw were quite different.

Many of these thoughts bothered Amy, who had definite goals of her own. She wanted to become a dancer and a writer and she eventually accomplished her wishes. She also became a professional singer. Bruce had no sympathy for her ambitions. Bruce said she would be fulfilled in helping him reach **his** goals. He gave her a very special ring that had been his grandmother's. He was going back to Hong Kong at the end of the semester and he wanted to announce that they were going to be married, but she said she did not want to be "a lotus blossom" to him. Still, she had trouble refusing him. She was offered a summer job in the Asian

pavilion at the New York World's Fair and it was to last six months. Bruce was aware of the job offer and he pushed her into a position of accepting or rejecting his last marriage proposal. Amy took the job and disappeared. Bruce tried unsuccessfully to find her. He left for Hong Kong in an angry mood.

During that courtship period with Amy, Bruce would, from time to time, go to Garfield High School with his Japanese girl friend to speak to the Chinese philosophy class. Bruce could teach without a credential because he was a guest lecturer brought in by an accredited teacher whom he knew. On one of these occasions a blond, athletic girl of 17, Linda Emery, saw him at the end of the hallway and asked her Chinese girl friend, Sue Ann Key, the very same question all the girls were asking. "Who is **that**?!" Sue Ann had taken ballet and dance and had, because of these studies, come into contact with Bruce at the University of Washington. "That's Bruce Lee," she said, "Isn't he beautiful?!" Everyone agreed. Sue Ann explained that Bruce taught a form of martial arts and named a couple of styles which meant nothing to Linda or anyone else. When Bruce would make appearances at Garfield High, the word would quickly get around and echo among the girls. "That Bruce Lee guy is here!" and the girls would find a way to impede his progress toward the room holding the Chinese philosophy class.

Linda said, "He was 23 and gorgeous. He would come to Garfield in a black, Italian, Hong Kong suit with a purple shirt and a skinny black silk tie, his hair slicked back and a curl kind of coming around his forehead. Even the lining of his jacket was purple silk. He looked like he had just walked out of **West Side Story**, which was playing about that time. George Chakiris is

Taky Kimura was 20 years older than Bruce, but that never got in the way of a lifelong friendship. Taky was Bruce's business manager, confidant and training partner.

what he looked like to me. He was suave and debonair and big city." Linda had no chance to meet him at Garfield High School and she concluded, "I don't say I thought about him all the time but certainly once in awhile! When he would come to the school I guess I was gog-eyed. All the girls were."

Bruce never noticed Linda Emery among the throngs of admiring girls, nor could he have known she would play such an important and final part in his life.

In addition to his teaching, Bruce and his entourage were giving exhibitions everywhere in the Seattle area, trying to make a little money and gain converts. Jim DeMile relates what happened at one ill-fated performance. "We had routines that we did at exhibitions, like appearing on television and sometimes we'd get confused. Things might fall apart, no matter how much Bruce rehearsed us. I remember that I ended my routine facing in the wrong direction and with my face against the rear curtain of the stage. Bruce would start to boil. And then Jesse (Glover) or Leroy (Garcia) would get mixed up. Bruce would hiss, 'Fake it, they won't know the difference!' And you could see that Jesse was slowing down because he was forgetting the routine and then he stopped to stare at Bruce and Bruce got very mad. But Jesse was very much like Bruce. There was always an unpredictable streak of violence to Jesse and he was tough, and Bruce liked that. But then, right there on stage, he suddenly hit Bruce. No reason except for all those lights and the heat and everybody sweating and he had forgotten what he was supposed to do. The transformation of Bruce was electrifying. And we're on television. Bruce stared at Jesse for a few seconds as the anger built and then he smashed Jesse in the face and flattened him. We dragged him off and I think the people in the control booth thought it was part of the act and a fine way to end the whole thing."

This sort of thing happened several times and Bruce hated to be hit. He had a fear of being knocked out because of his size. In the United States he was going up against men totally different from the small fighters he encountered in Hong Kong. In Hong Kong he fought against 135-pounders measuring maybe 5-feet-5. Now he had to contend with 200-pounders standing six feet and more. Here he was dealing with "trucks rolling in." DeMile says, "During a demonstration I really tried to hit that fella. When he hit you it hurt, so when he'd say, 'Try to hit me,' I really tried because I knew if I did hit him I'd get even. He was tiny. But I never could. He was good at traps. You started to make your moves, bobbing and weaving and jabbing, and he'd suddenly trap your hands, or pin them against your body. He was very frustrating. We were so stupid that we didn't understand his concept of fighting. We were ripe meat for Bruce." The gang challenged him more as they got better, but Bruce improved, too. The gang, in their rough ways, helped Bruce increase his speed and power. Because of the gang's growing expertise, Bruce started to evolve a beautiful series of motions and controls that were missing from his repertoire when he first came to Washington. In the beginning he could easily beat these streetfighters because they were so awkward. But they became more skilled and refined in their techniques, thanks to Bruce, and he had to grow to stay ahead. Bruce was growing intellectually as well. He was seriously studying and dissecting all forms of fighting to find what he could utilize and adapt. This was not done superficially. He became an absorbed student of all martial arts techniques and attitudes, along with physical tools used in other sports, such as football and basketball. As the streetfighters progressed on a physical level, Bruce was matching and surpassing them, while adding to his store of knowledge. He was beginning to soar. He was possibly one of the few conceptual martial artists who ever lived. He broke down all the martial arts and rebuilt them with improvements. He would say, "It's good, but it needs restructuring." He reworked the structural nuances and then practiced the movements until they worked beautifully and effectively. He would make them work in a practical sense, refusing to stop with theory, written words or sketches. Bruce Lee might be remembered more as a conceptual martial artist than a fighter. He invented techniques that to this day have not been totally absorbed. In some ways he was the only one who could perform them.

It is much like a brilliant pianist writing an extremely demanding piece of music that only another brilliant and gifted pianist can truthfully perform. Yet he was impatient with everyone. He felt if he could make a certain move, then any trained person could do it simply by following his example. Contrary to the common perception, Bruce hated to teach. He did not suffer fools lightly. Whatever you got from Bruce as a pupil you had to take. He would demonstrate moves once or twice, but a pupil had to gather it all in very quickly and wrench loose whatever he could, because there would likely not be another chance. Many of his pupils have said that if you did not pick up things immediately he would dismiss or dump you. In some ways the pupil was more a puppet who was not so much a person he taught, but from whom **he** learned. He liked pupils who were good enough to test him. The pupil had to be a quick-read. DeMile says, "You got only what you took from Bruce. It was a shame that he didn't allow himself to be used in a manner that permitted others to gain from their sifu and his immense knowledge and learning."

Bruce's moods were wide and subject to sudden change. He could be a serious sage one moment, then tell a raunchy joke the next. Bruce stuttered quite often, an affliction he learned to control. Taky remembers a day when he introduced Bruce to a friend who had a similar problem. When Taky's friend began to stutter, Bruce thought he was being mimicked. His fists tightened in rage

and Taky thought Bruce was going to knock the man down before Taky hurriedly explained the problem. But Bruce was only partly mollified, aware that the man's condition painfully underscored his own problem.

Taky went with Bruce to stage an exhibition in California for the Ed Parker tournament. They were going through their routines and Bruce told Taky to hit him, which he often demanded of his students. But Taky says someone Japanese cannot bring himself to do that because of the respect a Japanese has for his sifu or teacher. Utmost respect must be shown at all times. "Besides," Taky says, "I would never have been able to lay a hand on him and I couldn't bring myself to try." Finally, when goading failed, Bruce suddenly reached out and slapped Taky's face. Taky's temper flared and he waded in toward Bruce, swinging at him with both fists. Bruce, surprised, backed up and fell over a box on which he had been sitting. Taky thought, "Oh God, this is the end of my life. I'm dead." But Bruce just laid on his back and laughed, yelling, "That's it! That's what I want you to do!"

The gang would often hang around the rear of Taky's store where the produce was stacked, "bullshitting and working out." The guys always knew when there was a girl around because Bruce's personality completely changed and Bruce would find it necessary to pick on DeMile. He recalls, "You knew when a girl was nearby. His whole demeanor changed. We would be joking and horsing around and suddenly Bruce would get serious and stand up and sure enough we'd look around and here would be a girl. Then he'd start talking to us as if he were **lecturing**. He was going to impress this girl. And he would say, 'Now, in my system what I do is...Ah, Jim, come over here.' And I'd think, 'Oh, Jesus,' and there was no way out and I knew I was going to get it. He usually picked on me because I looked more ferocious than the other guys. I made a better villain, which impressed the girl even more. Bruce would say, 'Now, Jim DeMile here was a champion boxer.' He'd build me into superman and then destroy me. He'd start showing off his moves and bouncing me off those lettuce crates. It got so if I saw a girl coming along I'd sneak away and disappear."

Taky was always available to Bruce's whims and wishes. Bruce had set a date with a girl who lived in Bellview, which was some miles from Ruby's place, and he called Taky to propose that Taky pick him up, then drive to Bellview for the girl so they could go to a movie. Taky did as Bruce proposed, then returned to retrieve them at 1:30 a.m. "I was like a chauffeur," Taky said, "and I didn't even dare look over into the backseat."

Another demonstration had Taky and Bruce staging a fight with two young Chinese students who had been thoroughly rehearsed. During the demonstration Bruce made some extemporaneous remarks to the audience and showed a couple of moves that had not been rehearsed, which, in turn, threw off the timing and cues of the Chinese students. One of the young men became rattled and promptly hit the other. Suddenly the well-oiled presentation started falling apart and they started to fight for real. It erupted into a brawl and Bruce hauled them backstage where he delivered a tongue-lashing. He was furious and embarrassed with the way their professionalism had dissolved.

Bruce had all the equipment to do the things few could do and he insisted everyone was equally capable if he only concentrated. When Taky could not keep up with him, Bruce would sometimes insult his friend. On a couple of occasions Taky told Bruce he was quitting because he could not do what Bruce wanted him to do. He wanted Bruce to find someone else. He told Bruce that it came easy for the teacher, but not the student. Bruce would not apologize, nor could he ever apologize to anyone. The closest thing to an apology was to suggest that Taky "had the talent, but refused to recognize his gifts." It was Bruce's way of mending confrontations.

Years later, during emotionally trying times, Taky considered suicide. Three times after the sudden deaths of his brothers and the weight of the family business being his alone, without so much as a warning he contemplated suicide. Further strain came from his divorce. He feels if he had not had the training with Bruce and his view of life he would not have survived the difficult times. Bruce would hear of Taky's trials and call from wherever he might be in the world to bolster his friend, ending with, "Walk on, Taky. Just walk on."

Bruce returned to Hong Kong in some disarray, having seen his romance with Amy Sanbo dissolve. He rejoined his parents, his sister and brother Robert, a servant, a cousin, an aunt and a chicken in a bird cage. He was joined by another American, Doug Palmer, who had become one of Bruce's students in Seattle. Palmer later became an attorney and currently practices law in Seattle. He saw Bruce performing at a street fair in Seattle around 1963 and became a disciple. Bruce invited Palmer to Hong Kong in 1964 and he joined him in the crowded conditions of 218 Nathan Rd., Kowloon. It was then that Bruce renewed his relationship with the actress Pak Yan and taught her "how to be a bad girl."

Palmer, whom Bruce called "Baak Ma Dak," which means "White Horse Doug," recalls that summer in Hong Kong with Bruce: "When I stepped off the plane at Kai Tak Airport the first thing I noticed was the smell, followed almost immediately by the sweltering muggy heat, like stepping into a giant sauna. Hong Kong definitely had an odor that was distinctive: a thick tropical salt air suffused with a stew of smells that hinted at exotic foods, rotting garbage, human sweat, nightsoil and traces of things one couldn't identify. By the time we got to the Lee's apartment suite on Nathan Road my nose had grown accustomed to the smell, but the muggy air drenched my entire body in beads of sweat all summer long.

"The ride from the airport was exhilarating, through narrow streets of pushcarts and lorries and weaving taxis, between tall narrow tenements and office buildings with crowded shops at street level, and colorful signs in Chinese characters that stuck out from the buildings, fighting for space over the sidewalks. Swarms of people filled the sidewalks, sitting in front of shops, standing at sidewalk food stalls, coolies in undershirts and old ladies in black pajamalike pantsuits rubbing shoulders with businessmen in Western suits.

"The Lee's apartment was anything but ostentatious. It was on Nathan Road, past the Gurkha barracks away from the Star Ferry, right across from the Shamrock Hotel. It was on the second floor of an old building of several stories, above some shops. The narrow stairway leading up to the second floor had no door at the bottom. At that time Hong Kong had recently suffered a mass influx of refugees from the Mainland, and housing was at a premium. Shantytowns had sprung up, families built shelters on the roofs of buildings and people slept in parks and on the street. One fellow had staked out the landing halfway up to the Lee's apartment as his pallet at night. Every evening we came home late we would have to be careful to step over him in the darkened stairway.

"Like many apartments in Hong Kong then as now, two doors guarded the Lee's apartment on the second floor landing: an outer one of stout bars like a jail door, and a thick inner one with a peephole. The inside consisted of a number of sparsely furnished rooms. Most activity took place in the large room with a refrigerator at one end. It tripled as a dining room, living room and sleeping area. The household gathered around the dining table not just for meals but for games, conversation, and reading. Bruce also set up the ironing board in this room when he ironed his pants or shirts. He was meticulous in his dress and did not think the women in

the house were able to properly iron his clothes. Along the wall beside the table was the bed Bruce used. The beds all consisted of frames with hard mats on them, more like sleeping platforms. In the oppressively muggy Hong Kong summer, no bedclothes or blankets were necessary. A fan was also set up in the room to relieve the still, stale air.

"Beyond the dining room was a smaller room that overlooked Nathan Road, with two beds, one used by Bruce's younger brother and one by me. Alongside the dining room was a room of about the same size that held two doubledeck bunks. Beyond that, also overlooking Nathan Road, was a veranda with a makeshift bathing area curtained off on one side along with numerous potted plants. The bathing area was needed because the tub in the bathroom, owing to the drought, was kept filled with water used for cooking and flushing the toilet.

"The drought that summer did not make things any easier. The water was on only a few hours every fourth day, at which time the bathtub and every other receptacle in the apartment was filled with water. To take a bath, one took a small bucket of water to the curtained-off corner of the veranda and sponged off: Not that it did that much good, since one was drenched in sweat again within minutes of bathing, but it made you feel a little bit better for a short while.

"Bruce made constant efforts to educate me in the nuances of Chinese etiquette. But try as he might to anticipate the more gauche lapses of his gwei-lo friend, he was up against an obtuseness that was nearly impermeable.

"At the first meal at the Lee table I trotted out my best manners. The first course was a soup of clear broth and some vegetables. I sat up straight, raising my soup spoon to my mouth and taking care not to slurp. Eating silently is not considered complimentary. After a few minutes Bruce leaned over and whispered in my ear, 'Make a little noise.'

"He also took delight in faking fights

with me in front of Chinese onlookers. We practiced our routine: two roundhouse swings from me which he blocked with his forearms, then a stiff uppercut to my stomach which I had to make sure I tightened in time. We would time it so that we would emerge from an elevator arguing loudly, then swing into our skit in front of the crowd waiting for the elevator.

"For some reason Bruce's father had determined that Bruce should, at age 22, get circumcised. One afternoon, a week before we were to leave for the States, Bruce returned to the apartment with a halting, tentative, bowlegged walk, as if he had a 'load' in his pants. He quickly changed from the tight pants he normally wore to loose-fitting Chinese pants he borrowed from his father. Then all the men in the family crowded around to inspect the surgeon's handiwork. There was a symphony of sympathetic ex-clamations when Bruce gingerly displayed his swollen purplish penis in his hands. Every morning after that until we left we would all conduct an inspection to note the progress he was making. By the time we took off he was able to walk almost normally.

"I'm not sure whether Bruce's sense of humor was Chinese, or whether it was uniquely his own, but his practical jokes did not seem to depend on the victim's ever knowing his leg had been pulled. In those days, when he was getting into a lot of trouble, he sometimes would act like an 'uncoordinated nerd and let a street punk goad him. When the punk swung, Bruce would block it awkwardly and snap a fist into his groin with an incapacitating blow that appeared like an accident. As the punk rolled in pain Bruce would cover his mouth with his hand, tittering like a fairy, and swishing off. 'A person can accept getting beaten by someone who is stronger or bigger than he is,' Bruce would explain, 'but if he thinks he's been beaten by a "girl," he'll be pissed off for the rest of his life.' "

The summer was closing and Bruce and Palmer had to get back to the United States. Palmer was off to college in the East and Bruce was to begin a fall term at Washington.

Too, Bruce would start his own wing chun classes at the Jun Fan Kung Fu Institute.

Chapter Four

Linda

In the late summer of 1963, Linda Emery, accompanied by friend Sue Ann Key, joined the Bruce Lee School of Gung Fu which was held in a tree grove in an isolated area on the University of Washington campus. Linda was to become the most influential part of Bruce's life and harbor him from the many vicissitudes that marked Lee's short, roller-coaster life. Bruce had just come back from Hong Kong, where he had gone after the bitter and frustrating courtship of Amy Sanbo. He lost himself in what he did best: work. He was compared to a tightly wound armature of a powerful motor. He could not relax or allow himself time that was not guarded or alert. Linda's calm nature was well suited for someone of Bruce's volatility.

Linda and Sue Ann paid only a few dollars for their tuition and Linda expected to be bored with the whole exercise, except for the proximity of her teacher. The group met every Sunday morning and Linda discovered it to be a great deal of fun. She was so engrossed in the training she became a fervent convert. After the Sunday meetings the group would go to Chinatown for lunch. There would be 12 or more and Bruce would lead the group in gorging itself, gesturing furiously with his chopsticks. Linda had never had Chinese food with the exception of egg flour

"You'll never find anyone like her."

soup and it was a new experience. "I put sugar in my Chinese tea and I thought Bruce would choke when he saw that. But now I can't go long without getting back to Chinese food." Then some of the group would go with Bruce to an afternoon film and once they saw Bruce as a 5-year-old, performing in the Chinese film, **The Orphan**. Bruce preferred Japanese samurai films and he would come out of the theater to mimic the lead actor, swinging a wooden slat and looking better than the samurai himself. He would often deliver a critique of all the action and point out where it could have been improved. It was the summer that Linda was falling in love.

Some of the classes he took at the University of Washington at that time were theater speech, drawing, social dance, basic speech improvement, leadership lab and Chinese philosophy. He was very conscious of his accent, which was, at times, amusing to the Western ear.

Linda also joined the gang in its endless public exhibitions. Taky said, "She was really very good. She was a good athlete and learned quickly." In class Bruce often used her as a foil or asked her to perform a move. They appeared before fraternities, sororities and various clubs, trying to interest students in Bruce's classes. He would ask a young man to come up on stage to take him on. The athletes found it to be something of a joke, considering his size. Football players loudly and openly scoffed at his challenges, but Bruce would pick out a particularly large player and have him come up to try his luck. Bruce would flick out a hand that could hardly be seen and come within a quarter of an inch of the player's nose. Then he would step back and kick out to graze the man's nose again and the man would touch his nose with wonder, feeling only the wind. Then Bruce would deliver a short punch to the man's shoulder that would send the 250-pounder reeling in a heap across the stage. Bruce would try another volunteer, telling him to hold his arms at his sides, as Bruce

was doing, and then tell him that he would touch the man's cheek with his hand. The man should try to block the move, he suggested. He would ask the man if he were ready and the man would nod. Bruce would tap the man on the cheek and return his hand to his side before the man had started to lift his arm. The man would often say, "Wait a minute. Let's do that again." Bruce would make them look like real bumblers and humble them before an audience.

Still, not all these performances went well. Taky vividly remembers participating in a show on the educational channel, Channel 4, when Bruce misjudged the distance Taky was standing from him. Bruce was looking toward the camera and lecturing, when he threw a punch and smashed Taky's glasses while trying to emphasize a point. Blood poured from Taky's eye and dripped from his chin. Glass was imbedded in his eye. He was rushed to the hospital and the doctor scolded him for taking such fool chances. Taky had never worried because Bruce was so accurate with his punches. Yet, Bruce felt it could not be his fault. He accused Taky of having moved. He said that Taky had moved an inch. Taky said, "You're right, Bruce. I moved." Taky knew he had **not** moved, but such was their relationship. Taky had to wear an eye patch for a couple of weeks. Understandably, Taky became a little gun-shy of Bruce, a little afraid of what might happen the next time. Bruce's lightninglike kicks to Taky's groin would touch the cloth of his jeans, but fortunately nothing else. Bruce even started demonstrating the use of the dangerous nunchaku, each time missing Taky's face by an inch.

As one of his friends in Seattle said, "He was a voracious and non-stop talker and the subjects were always the same. Bruce Lee and gung-fu. This could wear on even the most loyal of his friends and students."

When Bruce became famous he began his withdrawal from the public eye, but the years preceding that could only be called his period of exhibitionism. In the center of a crowded dance floor, Bruce was known to start doing one-finger push-ups until an audience formed around him. He loved the attention and adulation and murmured* praise, and even the awe his "shows" created. No matter what event, no matter how small, Bruce would not settle for secondary status.

The gang would meet on campus at the student union building that everyone called The Hub, taking over a part of the cafeteria for hours to eat and talk and watch Bruce leaping about to demonstrate this idea or that, always moving, gesturing and jumping up in excited animation. All the while he would tell jokes or recount humorous incidents and Linda remembers him as a great storyteller. Sometimes Linda would cut classes to join the group. When the weather was mild they would meet in the glen that had long been their favorite rendezvous. Linda remembers the Japanese girl Bruce had often been seen with no longer seemed to be a part of his life. "I always wanted to find her and thank her," Linda says. These sessions were often quite informal with Bruce going from one student to the other and pointing out flaws and fallacies. At one point, and for some forgotten reason, Linda ran to get away from Bruce. "I was probably being rather silly and coy," she says. The mating dance? In any case he caught up with her far down the field from the others and tossed her on her back to ostensibly lecture her on an obscure point of Chinese philosophy. He hovered over her and asked her to dinner. Go to dinner? Did he mean everybody? Because the group often went out together. "No," he said, "Just you." Linda said, "Obviously I said yes and we went to the restaurant at the top of the Space Needle which had been constructed for the Seattle World's Fair. It was very fancy and I never thought I'd see the inside of the place because it was so expensive. I had to borrow a dress from Sue Ann because she was more sophisticated

than I was and had nice things like that."

At dinner Linda did not check out the entrees so much as look over the prices, something she says she still does. Bruce gave her a present at this first dinner, a small doll whose hair he had braided to resemble Linda's hair when she came from swimming class. Linda's mother knew nothing of her date with Bruce and Linda knew she could not tell her. She had to sneak out or tell her mother she was going out on a double date, when she and Bruce started regularly seeing each other. In high school, Linda had dated a boy who was half-Japanese and her mother forbade Linda from seeing him again. He simply was non-white. Linda was brought up Protestant, going, for a time, to Presbyterian and Baptist churches, though her family was not especially pious. "We said grace on Thanksgiving and Christmas," Linda said, "and that was about it." Bruce had no contact with any church, and when asked if he believed in God he said, "To be perfectly frank, I do not."

They had been dating for six months during the football season when the University of Washington won the PAC-8 title and would be going to Pasadena for the Rose Bowl game on Jan. 1, 1964. Linda told her mother she was going to the game with a group from the university. "We didn't go to the game. To heck with the game. Our friends went, but we went and stayed with Ed Parker and his wife."

Bruce asked Taky what he thought about the idea of his marrying Linda. Taky said, "Bruce, you've got a gem there. You'll never find anyone like her. She's got more going for her than any girl you'll find again." Taky added later, "Her parents didn't have much use for him, but I don't think Bruce would have gotten as far as he got, or succeeded as much as he did without Linda." Bruce was an explosive man who barely suppressed his volcanic nature. Linda laid a cool hand on him at the proper times, turning the rolling

boil to a simmer. Bruce never operated at less than a simmer.

Bruce's love of raunchy jokes and terrible puns, usually at the expense of gwei-los, (foreign devils) is well known, but none could remember an example of his humor until a letter was received from Thomas Chan, an actor who played with Bruce in **Fists of Fury**. A Bruce Lee joke: Four gwei-los were sleeping in the same bed when one of those in the middle woke up, wishing to spit. He didn't want to disturb the others by getting up, but he noticed that the bedroom ceiling was quite low. So he spat up at the ceiling and the phlegm stuck to it. This over, he fell asleep again. Later, he had to spit again, but the phlegm did not reach the ceiling, falling back and into the open mouth of the qwei-lo next to him. Everybody woke up as the offended qwei-lo started yelling and scolding the first man. But the first man insisted that he had not wanted to spit in the man's mouth and he pointed up to the ceiling to show what he had done the first time. The other three qwei-los made a suggestion. The next time the man had to spit he should yell and the men would know what to do. That settled, they all went back to sleep. Suddenly the man in the middle shouted a warning and the other three quickly pulled the covers over their heads. Only, this time, the man farted.

Bruce badly wanted to get away from Ruby's restaurant. He felt as if he were suffocating and his anger deepened. Every Saturday morning, before the restaurant opened, Bruce would work out with the gang inside the restaurant. Ruby would "stare daggers," but she never threw them out. Taky says, "It seemed like everything she said kind of pushed Bruce into the ground. He wanted to get out of the restaurant in the worst way. So I suggested that we form a club and have the group pay him something for lessons so he could quit Ruby's. He quit and found an apartment on University Way and our new club paid dues that went to support him." Those same Saturdays found

Bruce teaching a troop of Chinese Boy Scouts in a hall in Chinatown. His love of children was a character trait that remained to the end. Bruce often taught the Chow children in the rudiments of wing chun in the back room. And he often played a game that always confounded them. They would blindfold him and make a circle around him. Then Bruce would say, "Try to touch me. One at a time." They would begin in random order, and as quietly as they could, make their moves. But he always managed to grab out and catch them before he could be touched. He would stand very still and hyperalert, seemingly to feel, hear, or sense someone coming toward him.

About this time Bruce ordered a wooden practice dummy, called a "mook jong," from Hong Kong. When it finally arrived he set it up under the stairway on the first floor and religiously practiced every morning.

Taky, as the only officer of the new club, collected the money, paid the bills and kept general order. Even later, when Bruce left for Oakland to open another school, Taky sent him the proceeds because he knew Bruce was barely making ends meet. "Some people thought I was crazy to do that, but I knew that Bruce had done more for me than I ever could repay," he said. This despite the injury to his eye.

Bruce had been thinking about starting a nationwide string of wing chun schools, but was leery because he did not want to have inadequate instructors trying to teach principles and techniques without close supervision. Also, as Taky says, "Many of the schools had very bad reputations for simply signing up kids for two or three years and taking their money without any thought of teaching." They decided to drop the idea.

The summer of 1964 had arrived and Bruce was going to Oakland to join James Lee and start the new school. Linda and he discussed the idea of her going with him or staying behind. "I decided to go," Linda

Bruce and Linda (far right) are shown at dinner with Bruce's brother, Peter, and his wife, at a Chinese restaurant in England.

said. "One of my better decisions." Bruce would first go ahead and get things settled and then she would join him. Linda said, "I even thought I might not see him again. I took him to the airport with Taky at the end of the semester. Bruce said he would come back, but I felt that the bottom had fallen out of my life, because you never know. His life could have taken a different turn, or he might begin to feel restricted. Who knows. He could change his mind." Linda rented a post office box so Bruce could write to her without the mail coming under the scrutiny of her mother or stepfather. In fact, Bruce proposed marriage by letter and promised to come back in August, which he did, with a ring he borrowed from James Lee.

Rather than dealing with Linda's mother and her family, Linda and Bruce agreed to run away and get married. Better to tell the family after the fact. Blood tests required they wait three days before marrying and as Linda ruefully remarked, "At 18 you don't know about things like the vital statistics page of your local newspaper." Who reads these things? Why, Linda's old, maiden aunt, that's who. She called Linda's mother, who was working at Sears at the time. Linda's mother marched up to the floor where Linda

was working, shook the newspaper in Linda's face and yelled, "What's this!? Is this you!?" The news had hit the fan.

"It was awful. It was awful for my family and it was just an awful way to do it." Her mother called a meeting of the family. It was a show of force that was designed to change Linda's mind. She got in everybody available. Two aunts, one uncle, her stepfather and grandmother. "They arrived on Saturday and we all sat around in the living room as if there had been a death in the family," Linda said. "It was awful. Bruce came to be with me and it was the first time any of them had met him, including my mother. This was a first introduction." Bruce had said, "I want to marry your daughter. We are leaving on Monday. I'm Chinese, by the way."

The thrust of the argument, at least in the beginning, was the obvious haste of the affair. They wanted Linda and Bruce to wait. Maybe a year. They refused to forbid her to marry a Chinese, not in front of him. They said she was too young, that Linda had just turned 18. They wanted to know what difference it would make to wait a spell. They asked how he was going to support Linda and what he did for a living, which, when they found out, made things worse.

55

"You teach what?" He might as well have told them he taught people how to turn purple. It was nonsense to them, as it would have been to most people. They did not **dislike** Bruce and they treated him politely. They were not rude, they just did not want him to marry Linda. What particularly hurt Linda was the attitude of her favorite uncle, who took her out for a drive and a long talk after the initial meeting. The uncle was quite religious and told her this marriage was not the Christian thing to do. He quoted something about the mixing of the races. It was his opinion, along with the opinions of other members of the family, that races should not mix. It was in the Bible. Linda was completely disgusted with that kind of argument. "I couldn't see," she said, "how these very nice Christian people could tell me that I could not associate with a person when I believed all other messages in the Bible you were supposed to learn from a Christian upbringing, which is the idea that all people are alike and to treat everybody alike. I had no prejudices. I was raised with racially mixed friends. I had no problems like that. Central High School was about 40 percent Black, maybe 40 percent White, and the rest Oriental." Before Linda got the post office box she kept Bruce's letters locked in a box in her bedroom. Linda discovered her stepfather had broken into the box and had read them, which he divulged at the family meeting. Bruce said, "Don't worry about it. Everything will turn out fine." Bruce understood why her mother was upset. Here was her baby leaving with an Oriental man who taught a thing called gung fu, with no visible means of support, to the rough town of Oakland and into a dubious future. Years later, however, she grew to love and admire Bruce.

When they could not dissuade Linda, they tried to talk Bruce out of the proposition; surely, he had more sense, being 24. Linda's mother said, "You know, Bruce, Linda doesn't know how to cook, clean or sew, or anything." Which was true, Linda says, because her mother always insisted on doing everything. Bruce said, "She'll learn." She did learn, but it came slowly. She did not clean the refrigerator the first year of her marriage. Finally she realized she was going to have to clean it, along with the stove. "It was a terrible awakening," she said, "a real letdown."

The first family meeting was Saturday. Sunday was worse. "A perfectly horrible day," Linda said. "This was the day of tears," It was awash with tears, but it made no dent in the couple's decision, so Mrs. Emery tossed in the towel by announcing if they were going to get married they had to get married in church. The family did not even go to church by this time. Linda's mother was the family historian and she was forever searching the family history. She wanted this event, as painful as it was, to be properly added to what she knew. She had records of who married whom, who died and where. It had to be properly recorded. Linda and Bruce agreed and someone got in touch with the minister of Seattle's Congregational Church. Taky was Bruce's best man, while only Linda's mother and grandmother were there from her side. They had arranged for the minister to preside in the chapel and Linda wore a brown dress. There were no flowers. It was all done very quickly to meet the Monday deadline, but Mrs. Emery said, "He could have bought flowers, anyway."

For about a year, Bruce took a new partner and established a second school to display his wing chun methods. The partner's name was James Lee, considered to be an extraordinary fighter and teacher. James Lee was 12 years older than Bruce and a part-time martial arts teacher. Linda said he was, "A laid-back sort of person and a kind, kind man." James was about Bruce's height with heavily calloused hands, thanks to his trade as a welder. He always appeared disheveled and his hair uncombed even when it was, and his clothes were rather ill-fitting. His specialty was "iron-hand techniques," breaking bricks and boards. Many of his techniques were so often considered stunts, and "fake stunts," but he could do them. He did not have to "bake the bricks" or "doctor the boards." He could do what he said he could do, which always appealed to Bruce. Bruce hated frauds and celebrated those who could "produce." James was subsisting in Oakland with a devoted wife and two children, 12 and 8. He and Bruce opened the door of the new studio at 3039 Monticello Ave., a thousand miles closer to Hollywood than Bruce had been, but it was a difficult time. They had few students and little income but for periodic checks from Taky in Seattle, and Linda was pregnant. "It was difficult, yes," Linda says, "but we were young and in love and it was exciting." They did not need much and they paid no house rent. The whole bunch could live on very little and James had a car.

Bruce and James had hardly set their "shingle" above the door when they were handed a scroll, written in Chinese, that demanded they take down their sign and stop teaching the sacred and secret Chinese fighting methods to foreigners. If he refused, the challenger, Wong Jack Man from across the bay in San Francisco, would come over and give him a beating. The loser was to close his shop. Bruce, of course, refused to shut down what they had just begun and a day was appointed for the fight. Wong arrived with several friends, most of them fighters. They all stood around in the small gym and declared that they came with a formal set of rules to govern the fight. There would be no kicking to the groin, jabbing to the eyes and other sundry tactics. A long list. Bruce refused again, his anger mounting. "You came here and challenged me to a fight to the end with one of us going out of business. Then it's no-holds-barred." There was some

hesitation with this, but Wong finally bowed, as did Bruce, and the fight began. Linda remembers the fight as being, "All out and very rough and not especially elegant." Soon Wong's entourage tried to step in to stop it because Wong was in trouble, but James waved them off with a scowl and the fight, brutal as it was, ran its course in about three minutes (long for a fight of this kind.) Much damage can be inflicted in that space of time. Bruce had Wong on the floor and was delivering a fine beating and demanding that Wong surrender. All this in screaming Chinese. Wong finally indicated he would quit and the group left without another word. The story of this fight has been talked and written about in books and many periodicals for several years, but none told of the true significance of the brawl. The fight was extremely important to Bruce because of the inordinate amount of time it took to defeat the man. He was annoyed with himself and he knew he had to once again examine his approach to fighting in the wing chun manner. He took a critical view of his methods and approaches to the martial arts. In public his view of himself was favorable to the egotistical; in private he was a fierce self-critic.

Linda thought the victory called for a celebration, but when she went to find Bruce he was sitting on the back porch of the gym, his head in his hands. Bruce was not in the least elated with the win. In fact, he was disgusted with his performance. He had expected to win, but it was the way he won that bothered him so. He knew how long it took to finish Wong and how exhausted he was at the end. His technique did not work as well against Wong as it had against others. And his analysis of the fight and his training and fight techniques came under close self-examination. Born from the fight was a new approach to kung-fu, which Bruce would later name jeet kune do. Realizing his limitations, he began to evolve his methods into the

famous "way of the intercepting fist," or jeet kune do. His classical movements were not effective against Wong's defenses or his back peddling. Much of wing chun's effectiveness lies in the proximity of the opponent. The techniques are especially damaging at close range and kung-fu fighters will remain within striking distance. All this changed for Bruce in the Wong fight and he decided to alter his training. He did not automatically say, "I'm going to blend a number of ideas into one fighting technique and call it jeet kune do," but the seed had been watered.

Many years later, after the story of the Wong fight had been told and retold in print, Wong claimed his character had been defamed and he had been held up to ridicule, which caused harm to his teaching of the martial arts. He sued Linda Lee, Danny Inosanto, and CFW Enterprises, Inc., for in excess of $1 million including punitive damages. The case was argued for two years before finally being dismissed. Many people would be proud to say they fought and lost to Bruce Lee.

Linda remembers a night when she and Bruce and James were in San Francisco and found themselves in the neighborhood where Wong worked as a waiter in a Chinese restaurant, "We kind of swaggered in to show ourselves. It was just like a scene from a movie. Wong was pouring tea for a customer and his eyes widened when he saw us and he kept pouring tea until the customer's cup was running over."

Bruce and James Lee, trying to make more money, wrote a small training book that sold in martial arts magazines. As the organization's secretary, Linda filled orders that came in at a good rate, which supplemented their scanty and unpredictable income. Students were still scarce and they charged those few little tuition.

Bruce always had good relationships with his students. He would always have time for them. They were always welcome, even years later. He was a friend, yet he was the teacher. In many cases, martial arts instructors place themselves on a pedestal and are unapproachable to their students. Bruce was just the reverse.

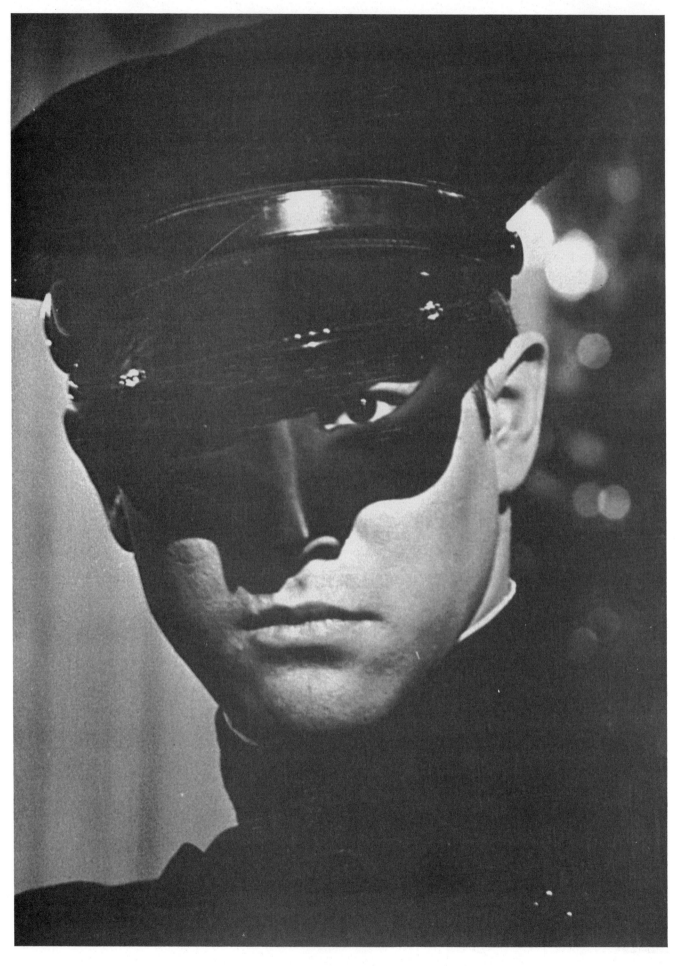

Chapter Five

Discovered

Jay Sebring, who later would be murdered along with Sharon Tate by the Charles Manson clan, owned an exclusive hairstyling salon in Beverly Hills. He had a seemingly contradictory interest in the martial arts. He practiced several Oriental fighting forms, exercised and went to Southern California martial arts tournaments. One fateful day he drove to Long Beach to view Ed Parker's 1964 Internationals. Bruce had been invited to the Parker event, and went with Linda to give an exhibition. What Jay Sebring saw astounded him and during the tournament was told that Parker had recorded Bruce's demonstration with a 16-millimeter camera. This kid, Bruce Lee, stuck in Sebring's mind. One of Sebring's customers was television producer William Dozier, whose credits included such series as "Batman," "Gunsmoke," and "Perry Mason." While Dozier was getting a shampoo and haircut, he mentioned he was looking for a young man to play a part in a proposed series called "Number One Son." The part called for an active, young, good-looking Chinese. Sebring told Dozier his search was over. He described this phenomenal spectral of a Chinese he had seen in Long Beach. And he told Dozier that Ed Parker had shot film of this lightning-fast apparition. Dozier could not resist the sales job and asked Sebring to

"It was great
while it lasted."

61

have Parker call him. Parker did, and was soon on his way to Dozier's offices at Twentieth Century Fox Studios with a tiny roll of film. Dozier saw the footage and immediately called Bruce in Oakland. Would Bruce be interested in testing for a part? He would. Could he see his way clear to get down to Twentieth? He could. Bruce tested well, but the series was declined by the networks and Bruce continued to teach in the small studio with James Lee. Tragedy soon struck when it was learned James' wife had inoperable cancer. She died two months later. They were all shattered and Linda suddenly had a family, the men and James' two young children. "I was learning to cook now," Linda said, "ravaging Betty Crocker's cookbooks. When I think back, my God, the things I fed those people." Only a few months later, Linda and Bruce had their first child, Brandon. Then Bruce's father died in Hong Kong. They knew that Bruce had to go to Hong Kong for the funeral. Linda decided to return to Seattle. The stay in Seattle proved difficult, what with Mrs. Emery still not ready to accept the situation. "Here I was," Linda said, "a babe in arms and my mother saying, 'How could you have done this?' "

In Hong Kong, Bruce not only paid last respects to his father as he lay in the mortuary, but performed penance as well. When a father dies, and the sons are not present at the death, ancient Chinese custom demands that they "come crawling back," either to where the father awaits burial, or to the grave in which he is buried. Or, in the case of cremation, to the urn that holds his ashes. Bruce arrived at the mortuary and crawled from the door to his father's casket, wailing as he went. He made peace with a man he did not like and hardly knew.

A famous trio. Bruce Lee poses for this shot with martial arts heavyweights Hayward Nishioka (left) and Chuck Norris, who would later star with Bruce in a film shot in Rome.

Bruce Lee is shown in two of his major roles. Opposite James Garner (top) in the movie *Marlowe* and as the masked "Kato" in the smash television series "The Green Hornet" (above).

Linda stayed in Seattle two weeks and then met Bruce in Oakland upon his return from his father's funeral.

William Dozier called again. He was offering a new series to the networks called "The Green Hornet," based on the comic strip. His latest series, "Batman," was in front of the cameras, but he was looking ahead, as producers do. The part was for the character, "Kato," the Green Hornet's side-kick. He would produce "The Green Hornet" if "Batman," a similar kind of story, did well, but they would not know for a year. If he produced "The Green Hornet" he would like to use Bruce. Would Bruce sign an option agreement for $1,800. Bruce would. Now they had $1,800 and a year to wait. Instead of teaching, Bruce decided they should go to Hong Kong. The air fare came to $1,800.

They lived in his parents' home on Nathan Road where Bruce grew up and started their year's wait by spending four months with Bruce's mother and several relatives. Because of her husband's death, Grace was depressed much of the time, though she accepted her new daughter-in-law, as did the whole family, if even in a standoffish manner. However, it was not the burning issue it was in the Emery household. Still, it was not "palsy-walsy," as Linda put it. "And they would have preferred that Bruce had married a Chinese girl. Not that Bruce was that close to his family. He wasn't."

Still it was a difficult time. Linda could not speak Chinese and Brandon was difficult. "Brandon was an awful baby," Linda says. "He cried all the time. Not sick, just ornery." No one would let Brandon cry, not the slightest peep. He was the first grandson and was born just before the grandfather died. No matter what time of night, Bruce's mother or sister would jump out of bed at the first whimper and walk the floor with him. To save them this trouble, and to maintain her position, Linda would have to attend to Brandon first. Linda was wearing out and

Brandon "became the number-one spoiled child you have ever come across."

Trying to smooth things, Bruce would often take the family out for Yam Cha, which is comparable to English teatime. Bruce was generous with the family and he and Linda took control of his mother's welfare.

Bruce began to brag about Linda's cooking. "She can cook anything. Just you ask. You ought to try her spaghetti sauce. Just ask." He went on and on and then everybody was after Linda to cook a spaghetti dinner. "Let's get her to make her wonderful spaghetti." The choice of beef in Hong Kong at that time was very bad and though they had canned tomatoes, they lacked canned sauce or tomato paste. She assembled all that she could find, but then she had never cooked on a gas stove. The first thing she did was burn the tomatoes. Everything was going wrong and the spices were wrong and then she found out that Bruce had invited all the relatives. Instead of cooking for four, she was to serve 20. "It was awful," she says, "just awful. They ate and smiled and made little murmuring sounds, but I could tell that they were sorry that Bruce was 'stuck' with me."

At this time Bruce had no interest in a Hong Kong film career and made no attempt to contact his former movie friends. It never occurred to him to go back into film in Hong Kong, though many of his former co-workers were still active in the industry. He took Brandon to see his old teacher, Yip Man, and had a picture taken of the old man holding the young son. There were details of his father's estate to be settled and he spent more and more time by himself, immersed in his thoughts. He also was concerned with providing for his family and started to feel the burden of a wife and child—a feeling that would grow. After four months they returned to the United States and stayed with Linda's mother, stepfather and grandmother in Seattle. Again they bedded down for a period of four months, but it was not pleasant.

"Brandon was screaming all the time," Linda says. "He was spoiled rotten by this time. He would cry and it would bother my grandmother and I would get up at all hours once again to walk with him so he wouldn't disturb her." Brandon would not sleep through the night until he was 18 months old.

During this time in Seattle, Bruce was interviewed by a couple of sportswriters, one of whom was John Owen, now sports editor of the **Seattle Post-Intelligencer**. He tells of Bruce sitting in the sports department and challenging them to play the game he often "worked" on men, his famous "dime grab." One of the sportswriters, and an athlete noted for his quick reflexes, agreed to pit himself against Bruce. Owen still marvels at what happened. The writer was asked to hold out his hand, palm up, and in it Bruce placed a dime. He then told the man he would remove the dime before the man could close his hand. The writer nodded and Bruce, staring at his subject, positioned his hand a few inches over the open palm. Suddenly Bruce moved and the man snapped his hand closed in a tight fist. He flashed a victory grin toward Bruce. He could feel the coin in his hand and he knew he had won. Bruce could only shake his head at the man's quickness and he innocently asked for his dime back. The man opened his hand to find that the dime was gone and in its place was a nickel. They shook their heads at this demonstration of truly amazing reflexes and precise physical dexterity.

Linda's mother knew they would not stay forever, but she wondered aloud when Bruce was going to get a **real** job. Bruce would say he had this "movie job coming up." And her mother would say, "Oh, yeah, yeah, yeah."

This was a period of technical gestation for Bruce, who melded many of his thoughts and experiences, while questioning his role in life. "There was much self-analysis," Linda said. "He became self-critical again because he felt that that would help him move

"The Green Hornet" provided Bruce Lee's big break into the world of Hollywood. Pictured above is Lee on the set of "The Green Hornet." At far right is friend James Lee.

forward again." What Bruce was doing was concocting a martial arts stew. The recipe included generous portions of wing chun kung-fu, Western boxing, Thai kickboxing, Greco-Roman wrestling, karate and more, some of it taken from direct experience and some pulled from the large library he had built related to the fighting arts. He watched movies of boxers Jack Dempsey and Muhammad Ali. He seasoned this with the teachings of Confucius, Buddha and Lao-Tzu. When he said his "style was no style," he meant it.

They had hardly settled in Oakland for a second time when word came that "Batman"

was a "smash" and "The Green Hornet" was next on the list. It was April, 1966 and Dozier's company would start shooting in June. The Lees rented a home in Los Angeles; it would be the first time they had lived alone since their marriage.

Bruce got his first weekly paycheck from an American film studio. He grossed $400 and took home $313.26. He and Linda were so thrilled they moved to Westwood, a beautiful suburb near Beverly Hills and home to UCLA. They took an apartment at Wilshire Boulevard and Gayle that looked "very English." Another move that reflected their newfound affluence was the purchase of their first automobile, a new, blue Chevy Nova for $2,500. But what Hollywood giveth, Hollywood taketh away. "The Green Hornet" succeeded enough to last one season, 26 episodes. Soon the Lees could not afford to live in Westwood so they moved to the Barrington Plaza, which they could afford even less. But Bruce had made an arrangement to give wing chun lessons to the manager for part of the rent. It was a large, two-bedroom apartment on the 23rd floor with a fine view. "It was great while it lasted," Linda said. They had been living there about six months when the apartment owners discovered that their manager had made a number of similar deals with tenants and he was canned. The Lees, along with several other tenants, were evicted.

Still, this was a good time for them. Kung-fu had never been seen on television, nor had there been much exposure in films, and the response was enormous. Many people were literally astounded by what they saw. Bruce got tons of fan mail and screen magazines were taking notice. His personal appearances around the country also were well received. Sometimes there would be six or seven stops a day—supermarkets, radio and television spots and newspaper interviews. Bruce loved mingling with the public one-on-one. He performed all his tricks and shticks for his fans and made a terrific impression with his sense of showmanship. He would call Linda every night, no matter how tired, and then have a few laughs with Brandon. His energy was inexhausting, but his back was beginning to cause him pain, an affliction that would grow worse and plague him the rest of his life. Still, his life grew more stressful, much of it self-inflicted. When he hit a lull, such as he was about to experience, it tore at him from within.

During the next couple of years his career drifted. He developed his martial arts, and particularly jeet kune do, to where he no longer wanted to teach. He maintained what he had grasped, modified and restructured

Bruce the chef. As dangerous as Bruce Lee was with his hands alone, could you imagine his skill with something as potent as a meat cleaver?

could not be learned from a book. He could not personally teach each student. His interpretation existed only in his mind and body. He realized if he were to "break out of the pack" it would have to be in film, and the thought drove him nearly insane.

Warner Brothers, in association with producer Fred Weintraub, was developing a pilot script called "Kung Fu" that they hoped would be sold as a series. If there was ever a vehicle made for Bruce, this was the one. Weintraub had met Bruce at a few parties and knew his talents. He called Bruce in for story consultations and concept talks, which were designed to give Bruce the inside track as the star of the series. Bruce was in Hong Kong when he received a telegram from Warners stating that the part had been awarded to David Carradine. Bruce was devastated. Here was a script with a Chinese background, with a Chinese in the lead role and based on the Chinese culture, and they gave it to a qwie-lo. The network, NBC, and various sponsors, felt a Chinese could not carry the lead role on American television. In retrospect, Bruce lucked out.

He was living, as fringe actors do, for the big one just around the corner. Small and bit parts sustain this brother and sisterhood. Bruce had a small part in a **Matt Helm** feature that starred Dean Martin and Sharon Tate. There were brief appearances in "Blondie," "Ironside," and "Here Come the Brides."

Bruce also had a number of "celebrity clients" whom he trained for as much as $200 per hour. This kept the family going during this difficult time.

Stirling Silliphant, who was one of Hollywood's most highly regarded writers, and the writer of **In the Heat of the Night**, **The Towering Inferno**, **Marlowe**, **The Poseidon Adventure**, and many others, had become one of these students. Steve McQueen, James Coburn, James Garner, Lee Marvin and Kareem Abdul-Jabbar also were members of this distinguished group. Silliphant wrote and produced a picture called a **A Walk in a Spring Rain**, which had Ingrid Bergman and Anthony Quinn heading the cast. The film was to be shot in Tennessee, and aware Bruce was struggling, Silliphant arranged for Columbia Pictures to hire Bruce as fight coordinator. He also wanted Bruce close at hand so he could continue his three-times-a-week training routine. Silliphant said, "The two stuntmen on the picture, who were real Hollywood red-neck types, wondered why I brought this little Chinese guy along. They had never heard of Bruce Lee and who was this guy to teach them how to fight. 'Shit, we'll kick his ass.' Their attitude was very wrong so I took them aside and told them that this little guy, pound for pound, could rip lions' asses, so you better not mess with him. They said, 'Shit.' So I told them that we'd have to clear this thing up because they'd be working for him and this wasn't going to help my film, so we'd better have a little demonstration. I didn't want anybody to get hurt, but I wanted to get a little respect for Bruce. So they said, 'Anything you want. Just give us a chance to show this little sonofabitch.' So I told Bruce about it and he said, "Yah, gotta straighten these guys out. No problem.' They went out to the swimming pool where Bruce had an airbag and chose the biggest guy first and had him stand about three feet from the edge of the pool, brace himself and hold the bag for protection. Bruce said, 'What I'm going to do is stand right in front of you and with no warning, no windup, no run, no nothing, I'm just going to kick. I'm going to hit the airbag you're holding, and you can get into any position you want to. I'll lift you from there out in the air and into the swimming pool!' 'Shit,' says the stuntman. So this guy gets into a kind of crouch, the two of them laughing when Bruce zapped him to catapult him nearly to the other side of the pool. He almost missed the water! The guy came up a Christian! Instant baptism! But the second guy wasn't convinced. He figured he was tougher than the first guy and it was just a lucky punch. Some kind of Chinese magic. So, he really gets braced, I mean he's like a linebacker. Bruce kicked and that sonofabitch almost missed the other side of the pool. He was up in the air and gone. Those two became slaves of Bruce. Bruce loved it. He loved doing things like that."

Bruce had never made many friends among the martial arts teaching fraternity. He had not endeared himself with the masters and teachers in the United States, insulting their cherished positions in both their fighting techniques and the ceremony of their myriad schools. Most were slavish in the way they clung to the classical methods and centuries-old teachings. Bruce ridiculed these moribund attitudes at every turn. Now his adversaries, these masters were not happy with heresies that were gaining their students' attention.

A small collection of his thoughts on this subject included: "The stances most students learn are worthless. They are just too artificial and mechanical and don't prepare a student for actual combat. A guy could get clobbered while getting into his classical mess. Classical methods, which I consider a form of paralysis, only solidify what was once fluid. Their practitioners are merely blindly rehearsing systematic routines and stunts that will lead nowhere."

And: "Why do people want to become students? Some want to lose weight. Some say they want to defend themselves. But I would say that the majority are there for one reason, vanity. It is exotic. They figure they'll learn Zen and meditation. I say that if you want something beautiful, you should take up modern dancing. What good would it do a boxer to learn to meditate? He's a fighter, not a monk. It's all too ritualistic, what with all the bowing and posturing. That sort of Oriental self-defense is like swimming on land. You can learn all the strokes, but if you're never in the water, it's nonsense. These guys never **fight**. They all want to break three-inch boards or two bricks, or something. Why? That doesn't make them fighters."

And: "I don't have a karate belt whatsoever. I think it might be useful to hold up your pants, but that's about it."

And: "Ninety-percent of Oriental self-defense is baloney."

And: "If you like colored belts go look at a rainbow."

And: "So many instructors just want to push the same old buttons and get you to react the same old ways. Over and over. You are a man, not a robot."

He was disdainful of those who stubbornly followed a particular school or style without question or challenge. Famous sensei Ed Parker said, "When he ridiculed people, he wasn't very tactful. He didn't pull his punches at all. You don't make friends by telling people their way of doing things is full of shit."

When he returned to Hong Kong he was equally insulting to the revered Chinese masters. He would spare no one when talking to the press or appearing on television. Kung-fu's ruling hierarchy rose defiantly against him. He appeared on a television talk show that included several well-known Hong Kong sifu. One of them rose, planted himself in a stance and challenged anybody to dislodge him. The other sensei approached him and pushed and shoved him, but none could move him. The sifu sneered at Bruce, waiting. Bruce got up and slugged the man in the face, sending him sprawling on his back. Bruce said, "Anybody can defend themselves if they dictate how they are to be attacked."

To this day in Hong Kong, many petty claims can be heard from these wounded, narrow individuals. They will say, "Lee was not Yip Man's **favorite** student," or "Lee did not even go to Yip Man's funeral." Some threats were more than spiteful, holding a more lethal message. There were reports and rumors of someone having been chosen to maim, or even kill, Bruce. These stories took on greater credulity when Bruce suddenly and mysteriously died.

Again, Silliphant said, "I was running every day. Bruce had me up to three miles a day. Really at a good pace, you know. We'd run the three miles in 21 or 22 minutes. Just under eight minutes a mile. So this morning he said to me we're going to go five. I said Bruce, I can't go five. I'm a helluva lot older than you are, and I can't do five. He said, 'When we get to three, we'll shift gears and it's only two more, and you'll do it.' I said okay, hell I'll go for it. So we get to three, we go into the fourth mile, and I'm okay for three or four minutes, and then I really begin to give out. I'm tired, my heart's pounding, I can't go anymore and so I say to him, 'Bruce, if I run anymore,' and we're still running, 'if I run anymore I'm liable to have a heart attack and die.' He said, 'Then die.' It made me so mad that I went the full five miles. Afterward I went to the shower and then I wanted to talk to him about it. I said, ya know, why did you say that? He said, 'Because you might as well be dead.' He said, 'Seriously, if you always put limits on what you can do, physical or anything else, it'll spread over into the rest of your life. It'll spread into your work, into your morality, into your entire being.' He said, 'There are no limits. There are plateaus, but you must not stay there, you must go beyond them. If it kills you, it kills you.' A man must constantly exceed his level, and boy, I said to myself so many times, that's what killed him. He killed himself, really. I don't know what the immediate cause was, but he drove himself through the ultimate degree of where he should go. I'm totally convinced of that. People ask me what did he die of? I say I have no idea. I know the principal that killed him, a brain aneurysm. But I don't know the physical factor. Here was a man that was such a perfectionist, whose drive for reaching his ultimate potential and going beyond it was so consuming. He said that to me in total sincerity, and died for it. But it's been a big lesson to me, because in a sense he's right, in a sense, but not to the point of obsession. He was obsessed."

Bruce used all the Chinese herbs and teas. Chrysanthemum and ginseng were his favorites; he placed great faith in ginseng for its reported cleansing and aphrodisiac qualities. The tea is made from the root of the ginseng plant that grows wild mostly in Korea. Bruce spoke of roots bottled in water, particularly those contorted into grotesque shapes with long beards, that sell for as much as $100,000. He described how the plant grows on the sides of steep hills and canyons that are very difficult to reach if they can be found. During the day they are hard to locate as they blend with other foliage, but at dusk they glow with an iridescent color and can be seen from the opposite side of the canyons. Centuries ago, the emperor's archers were trained to locate the plants from across the chasms, then fire a colored arrow at the plant so the next day other men could locate the ginseng plant. Some wealthy Chinese and Korean families were given their inheritance with ginseng roots that could be many decades old. They thought, as Bruce did, that ginseng has amazing curative powers. Bruce also believed in the medicinal qualities of queen bee honey, buying it in glass vials and breaking off the tops to drink the sweet liquid.

Bruce often performed a ritual he called "good morning exercises." He would place a weight on his neck, sometimes totaling 125 pounds, and then bend over at the waist again and again. On this particular morning in 1969 he had not warmed up sufficiently, or the weight chosen was too heavy. A careless thing. "His back didn't go snap, or anything like that," Linda recalls, "but he knew something was wrong and that he was in terrible pain." He went through extensive tests and it was determined he had damaged the sacral nerve in the lumbar region of his back. The doctor prescribed indefinite rest and then said most likely he would never again kick with either leg. Now, in the middle of a long, dry period, he fell prey to a painful and serious injury that would stalk him the rest of his life. The injury was psychologically as well as physically debilitating. They were living in a house they could not afford and even if he were offered work, Bruce could not perform. Medical expenses were growing and Bruce was ordered to remain flat on his back for six months. "We know what kind of guy Bruce was, all that energy. My God!" Linda said. She was busy with the children and Shannon was still a baby, but she had to get work outside the home for the first time in their marriage. Bruce found this very hard to accept and would not tell anyone. If he could not support his family it was a serious loss of face. A man was supposed to earn the money and the wife was to stay home and take care of the children. Bruce was still very Chinese in this regard. Linda, without any qualifications, had to find a job. Luckily, she got a job with a telephone answering service, which paid the minimum hourly wage. Now, for the first time, Bruce had to see to the children. His love for children could not be sustained for long periods, and now he changed his first diaper. He loved to bounce Brandon on his knee and hug his daughter, but his paper-thin patience soon tired of this activity. Linda worked from 3 p.m.-midnight. Brandon was in kindergarten and would come home before his mother went to work. Shannon was yet a year old. She would go to bed directly following 3 p.m. dinner and, they hoped, sleep. Bruce would look after Brandon until he went to bed at seven. Linda was losing weight. Bruce never told anyone where Linda went or what she did with her evenings. She would be off before three and if anyone called, Bruce would tell them she was shopping or visiting friends. Having an injured back and a working wife were disasters for Bruce. But they conspired to keep it all a secret. A year passed before Bruce's back showed noticeable signs of recovery. With money saved from Linda's job and some television residuals, Bruce decided to go to Hong Kong for a second time, this time taking only Brandon. He tried to give the trip a sense of adventure.

Chapter Six

The Hero Returns

Bruce was more of a hero in Hong Kong than he knew. "The Green Hornet" had been playing for some time and viewers there were enthralled that one of their own had been featured in an American television series. No one had ever done that before and his reception was a much-needed shot in the arm. He appeared on local television programs and he was interviewed by the press and talk shows.

During that trip to Hong Kong in 1970 Bruce had his boyhood friend, Unicorn, who was working for Shaw Brothers, probe the studio on his behalf for a possible film offer. At that time Sir Run Run Shaw was paying players 200 Hong Kong dollars a month, which broke down to $10 a week in U.S. currency. They all lived in dormitories on the lot and if you progressed nicely and your popularity rose, they gave you "wardrobe expenses." Bruce asked for $10,000. This sum was so large that at first they knew not how to respond. A proposal of $10,000 was so far from their experience they could only stare vacantly with the thought. Finally they laughed. Unicorn returned to Bruce with a proposal from the studio. Yes, they were interested in Bruce, and they were aware of his modest successes in the States, and because of their interest, they suggested Bruce play a part in an upcoming film for the

"You could see
he was a star."

75

generous sum of $75 dollars per week and "sign on" to be a part of their exciting company for seven years. If the public found favor with him he could expect to see his wages rise in leaps and bounds. In other words, he might, one day, make $200 a week. Bruce returned to America.

However a fuse had been lit in Hong Kong and the news media kept close track of Bruce though he was 7,000 miles away. Radio disc jockeys would call him in Los Angeles and leave their microphones open. Bruce said, "The media there kept in contact with me by telephone. Those guys used to call me early in the morning and even kept a conversation going on the air. So the public was listening to me."

One of those who was listening was Raymond Chow of Golden Harvest Studios, but more of that later.

Silliphant helped Bruce again when he wrote a part for Bruce in a script for the series "Longstreet," which featured James Franciscus. The role gave Bruce the chance to be taken seriously as an actor. Reviews of the show were mixed, but Bruce was given unanimous credit for "making" the show. Bruce's fan mail far exceeded that of the show's star.

Silliphant said, "I wrote the pilot script for "Longstreet" and I wrote it deliberately to star Bruce. He was still rankling after all this time from the "Kung Fu" thing with Carradine. This was before we went to India, this was between the two shows. The whole hour was devoted to one continuous lesson in jeet kune do and I took all the teaching Bruce had shown me. When it went on the air, the fan mail that came pouring in was all for Bruce. So much so that Tom Tannenbaum, who was then the head of Paramount television and a fan of Bruce's, demanded a six-to-ten picture deal for Bruce as a running character. He got a huge amount of fan mail, and it was because of that that Ted Ashley and Warner Brothers became interested in him. And some of the studios began to make

overtures. It also helped us with **The Silent Flute** because it showed Warners that he had star potential. Warners liked it, Warners in the persona of John Calley and Ted Ashley. Ted had studied a little with Bruce and they were all very fond of Bruce. They sensed he was a star but they didn't quite know what to do with him.

"The thing that fascinated me about Bruce was his real ability to entertain and come alive in front of people. You could see he's a star. You could see he had all the charisma, which most stars lack. Most stars can't entertain," Silliphant explains.

Bruce was in the heat of Thailand making **The Big Boss** when "Longstreet" aired later that year. The show was a great success and the critics raved about Bruce at the expense of Franciscus. It was very gratifying to Bruce to finally get some acclaim as an actor.

Silliphant also wrote the screenplay for **Marlowe** that starred James Garner. He developed one character especially for Bruce that showed his amazing athletic ability. As a piece of action it was a showstopper. Still, Bruce was not making much of a dent in the Hollywood scene. How many parts are there for a young, or old, Chinese? Coburn and McQueen helped him get small parts to keep him alive, and he worked as a fight choreographer on a couple shows. Bruce and Linda also felt a certain discrimination, or outright racism, from some. And his personality did not endear him to many. He had a tendency to, unguardedly, tell people what was in his head, no matter who he might insult, aggrieve or annoy. Though he had smoothed many edges, he would never be free of grievance and acrimony.

In 1968 the Lees bought their first home because everyone told them it was a fine investment, deducting taxes and interest on the loan. "But it doesn't matter if you can deduct money from your taxes in April," Linda says, "if you can't make your mortgage payments in October." They knew nothing of the costly property taxes and upkeep. Steve

His strength and agility were unmatched in the martial arts, even before he began incorporating different arts into his style of jeet kune do. Here you can see how high he could kick and how much strength it must have taken to lift his foe.

McQueen had his business manager judge it as an investment. He pronounced it sound and well located on Roscoe Mare Road near Mulholland Drive. The location was just fine for McQueen and Bruce, as Mulholland had always been a favorite "track" of car racers. "Good for the guys," Linda says, "but bad for children." They paid $47,000 for the house at about the time the IRS arrived at their newly won doorstep. Plus, their electric bills were running four times what they had been paying and other costs were mounting. Almost as soon as they bought it, they could not afford it. Then Bruce got a windfall. A building in Hong Kong that the Lee family owned was sold and Bruce's share was $7,000. This would relieve the stress of their financial situation, but, instead, Bruce bought a Porsche with the lion's share of the money. Now he could drive hub to hub with McQueen. "It was extravagant," Linda admits, "when we were hardly making mortgage payments. It was an extravagance, but it made Bruce happy."

Bruce had been running around with McQueen for some time, driving the twisting, canyon roads above Beverly Hills and Bel-Air. Bruce often would drive McQueen's car and these were happy times for him. He began to share McQueen's passion for speed and daring. It was another reflection of Bruce's need to do things in a hurry, almost as if he said, "There isn't that much time." Bruce's father had died at the age of 64, a year he had predicted in his youth, and Bruce had told people he would only live half that time. This proved eerily correct when Bruce died at 32. "He had to do everything faster and faster," Linda recalls. "It got to be an obsession with him, especially in the last couple of years."

Bruce's star rose like a Phoenix following his appearance as the mild-mannered servant with the deadly skills in "The Green Hornet." He also became a favorite instructor of the Hollywood set, teaching such luminaries as Steve McQueen, James Coburn, Kareem Abdul-Jabbar and Stirling Silliphant.

RUCE LEE

Chapter Seven

Silent Flute

One of Bruce's star pupils, Chuck Norris, would often visit them in their house off Mulholland, along with actor James Coburn. It was Coburn with whom Bruce found a "spiritual brother." Bruce was giving Coburn private lessons for $250 an hour. It was not so much the physical side of the martial arts that attracted Coburn, but the Oriental philosophy behind it. Sometimes, instead of working out, they would talk the entire session. Bruce and Jim were looking for the same level of understanding and they drew closer in their search of a shared vision. Out of it came a desire to make a martial arts film that relied heavily on a psychological structure. Bruce, for some years, had been "noodling and doodling" with an idea that later would become **The Silent Flute**.

Bruce was doing little film work at that time and filled his days by constructing a story that would make McQueen want to play the lead role. This would virtually assure its production because of McQueen's box-office status in those days. Bruce wasn't sure if he could write a full shooting script, so he devised an outline and took it to Stirling Silliphant. Bruce was to play several parts, portraying such diverse personalities and characters as a panther and a monkey. He would also perform very demanding physical feats.

"I'm not going to carry you on my back."

He lived for this film to happen. It was not only extremely important to him as a performer, but if he did not find work soon they would be in danger of losing the house. Much was being asked of this script.

Stirling Silliphant tells the story:

"What happened was that when Bruce had this idea for the film, which at that point was simply an idea and not a script, he wanted to do it with Steve McQueen, so we went to McQueen's house because Steve had studied with Bruce. Steve had taken basic stuff with Bruce, but he hadn't really stayed with it. As a matter if fact, he broke his ankle when he was shooting the **Thomas Crown Affair** because he was into the early stage of the martial arts when you feel very, very powerful, where you kick things because you feel so powerful. He kicked a car and it didn't move, but he did. So we talked to Steve, and I agreed if Steve would do it I would write it. Steve said naw, he was too busy and he couldn't get involved. Then on top of that he said, 'Let's face it, Bruce, this is a vehicle to make a big star out of you, and I gotta be honest with you, I'm not in this business to make stars out of other people. I love you, buddy, but you're just going to be hanging on my coattails and I'm just not going to do that. I'm not going to carry you on my back.' Outside, Bruce was in a rage and shook his fist at Steve's house and said, 'Someday, I'm going to be a bigger star than he is.' I never forgot that, we're standing in the courtyard of Steve McQueen's house, with Bruce looking up at the window, saying, 'I'm going to be bigger than he is.' He was obsessed with overcoming, and remember when you humiliate a man like that he never forgets. At any rate, we went to Jimmy Coburn. Now Jimmy is very spiritual—has gongs in his house—and he really understands Pharisees and Zen and everything like that. He's actually a Pharisee. He said. 'I'm with you.' So Bruce had this dream about a very mysterious martial arts character which was to be played by himself, and he appar-

ently had dreams about this for several years because he had many, many notes, and he came to me to ask if we could get a screenplay together. He saw this as his unique way to stardom because no one was writing parts for him and therefore he perceived, as do many Black, Asian, and other minorities perceive, that they have to create their own vehicles. No one is going to write it for them. By the way, the title is significant. **The Silent Flute** is the call of the heart, the call of the soul, and only certain people can hear it. Bruce would appear at different times in the story and he would be playing this flute, and you couldn't hear it, but monkeys could hear it, and different creatures could hear it, and by the end of the story the American guy, who is on this quest, hears it. And once he hears it he begins to achieve perfection. But in this quest there is a great deal of wonderful combat. So Bruce said, 'Would you write this?' I said, 'No. I'm up to my ears in work and I don't have time to do it.'

"Now Bruce is bereft. You have to understand his dream of this crazy film, and the trip to India, went on for two or three years. This was not just a passing fancy. It became an obsession; this was his road to stardom. **The Silent Flute**. Okay, seeing that he was in terrible financial condition, and because I loved him, and because of his teaching me to be a better person spiritually and physically, I said 'I'll write the goddamned thing. But I'm not going to do it alone while you guys are off fishing, so what we are going to do is the following: We are going to meet three nights a week in my office from 5-7p.m. I told Coburn that if he was shooting a film we'd go to him, but otherwise they were to come to my office. I would get my secretary in and we'd dictate scenes, dictate ideas, and we'd get it down. For about six months we had a period where

A happy crew enjoys the final moments of shooting for *The Way of the Dragon*. From left, Chuck Norris, Bruce, co-star Nora Miao and Hong Kong producer Raymond Chow.

none of us seemed to be out of town, and we met religiously. It got to be quite exciting, and Bruce and Jimmy contributed enormously and richly to the texture of the script. So that you could smell it. I mean it was there. That's why Bruce was so excited and we all got excited.

"We took it instantly to Warner Brothers and they instantly loved it. Then it came down to costs. The story called for locations all over Asia and even in Africa. They said we had to centralize it, and further, it had to be done in India where the company had great amounts of blocked rupees, or frozen funds.

"The rupees were sitting in India. You guys go over and figure it out. So it's very important to understand that the trip to India was the culmination of almost a year of working on this dream of Bruce's and we finally had 120-page script, the money and a 'go,' but we didn't have the right country. Warners wouldn't finance outside of India and they weren't willing to risk a greater amount of money. All through that trip to

India we constantly refined the script and tried to apply things we saw in India to it. The locations just didn't work. There were sequences that really had to be in certain locations which were not in India.

"I was a little overweight at the time. I said to Bruce, when we get to India, I said, do me a big favor. I want to lose 15 pounds on this trip to India. All I'm going to eat, to avoid being ill, is toast and tea, and certain cooked vegetables, and fish if they'll cook it the way I want. I'm going to avoid all their food and if you see me reach for anything else, I want you to give me the eagle claw, which is this thing here in the shoulder, you know, this is the way zebras attack you and they collapse your lungs when they bite. They bite into the shoulder. For some reason they invariably bite into the shoulder and people, some people, think they are horses with stripes, but they aren't. They are very dangerous animals. So this is a very basic attack. It's also an eagle attack. So I said, 'Give me the "claw" if I reach for anything fattening.' He only gave the claw once in

India, and it almost killed me. I went down screaming on the table with my face in my tea. I came back 15 pounds lighter.

"Anyway, we got on this plane and Jimmy and he were sitting ahead of me and I was sitting behind. It was first class cuz, thank God, we were flying for Warner Brothers then."

They traveled between 8,000-10,000 miles by air and chauffeured car, over remote dirt roads and through terrible heat. Bruce refused any suggestion that the trip was fruitless and hopeless. Silliphant and Coburn were very successful professionals with burgeoning careers and fine bank accounts, but Bruce had, literally, nothing. This was his only hope of breaking through and he would not let it go.

"We landed in Bombay, and then we flew to New Delhi and then we went all the way up to the desert in the north, to Pakistan by car. Now in the car, **Mr.** Coburn always sat in the front seat and Bruce and I sat in the backseat. Bruce had sort of a curious habit of humming pop songs under his breath, mile after mile, which irritated the hell out of Coburn. Coburn finally turned around to Bruce and said, 'For Christ's sake will you stop that. You're driving me crazy.' Bruce was crushed. I never will forget when Jimmy turned back, Bruce shook his fist at the back of Jimmy's head, and it started the friction between the star and the would-be star. It was that way all through India. The trip was horrible, dust, you know, horrible stuff. Long stretches of that. We were in the car hours and hours together. There would be humor and we would laugh, and then we would sleep, and then we'd talk about the film, and then there would be little anger spurts between the two of them. It began to be a pain in the ass. We were coming apart. Bruce and I got closer, Jimmy and Bruce got further apart. We went to Madras and then to Goa, which is way down to the south, and Bruce kept saying, when we were flying,

'Hey, it's beautiful down there. We can shoot down there.' We would point out to Bruce that you cannot get crews there, what do we do, parachute them into the jungles and mountains? Where are we going to put the generator? Where are we going to live? I mean, he had no idea of the production problems involved. So we get to Goa, and Goa at that time is a beach place overrun by hippies. When they saw Bruce, they fell in love with him. God knows how they knew him. They must have seen him in "The Green Hornet." They had to have seen him in different things. They **knew** him. Even there and then. More than they knew Coburn. These were white kids who were living like hippies in Goa, lying on the beach naked. It was an incredible period of time. They were German, American, French, Dutch, Scandinavian from ages 17-24. Young, hippie, beautiful people who loved film, and they invited us into their communes. We spent two or three days just hanging out there, talking to them. The point of the thing is that Bruce came alive and he started to entertain people. For example, we would go to airports and would have to wait. I'd sit there and wait, Jimmy would be reading something, Bruce would attract the kids. For some reason they would flock around him. The Indians had seen lots of white people, but they had not seen that many Asians, and Bruce was really a handsome man, as you know, and he would demonstrate in airports. Kicks, punches and kata for the kids. He would attract 40 or 50 young Indian boys around him, and they would stare at him with these brown eyes, and applaud.

"Then there was the day we were having lunch in a real out of the way, dumpy place and the food was inedible. Bruce had a couple lamb chops, which he couldn't eat. I remember Bruce throwing his food to a dog that had been watching us eat, and I'm talking about a dog that was starving, and the dog grabbed the piece of meat Bruce had

been eating. Instantly, from the kitchen, three Indian waiters came out with sticks and brooms and started beating the dog and took the meat away from the dog. Bruce was indignant and he was going to kill them, and Jimmy reached over and said no. The cook came over and said, 'Pardon me, Sahib, but you don't understand. Our children have no food, and to give it to a dog is wrong.' Bruce had tears in his eyes.

"He was suffering at the time, terribly from back pain. The final blow to him was the hotel room in Goa. He and I got really dumpy closets, Coburn got this suite. We left Goa and arrived back in Bombay, at the Taj Mahal, and Coburn had a suite that was three times bigger than this restaurant. I mean it was embarrassing, you could put an entire production company in the thing. Of course, he wasn't apologizing; he was a big star. I mean, this is his due, right? Bruce and I again had closets. Bruce was indignant. I mean this was the final blow and he was really angry about it. If anything, this trip steeled his determination never again to be dependent on people, or any Hollywood institution. It just reminded him of how far he had to go. In any event, both Jimmy Coburn and I had traveled, and extensively, in India. I was in total despair because I knew there was nothing in India that would match the locations of **The Silent Flute**. Bruce **knew** we would do it. Jimmy and I knew we would not. So we went out very heavyhearted knowing that this was his dream. When we got to India, and had gone everywhere, he got more and more desperate, saying, 'Well, let's go here, let's go there.' We did for a month. We kept showing him that India was a walked-over country. We took him up near the desert in Pakistan. You'd go out at dawn and the sand was covered with thousands of footprints and bus tracks no matter where you went. Suddenly from over the hill would come thousands of people. We kept explaining to him it's not going to work here. You could find rice fields on parts of

the coast, but they didn't even look like they look in Bali. And because Bruce had never traveled, he didn't know the difference. The result was when we came back from India he was truly in the depths of despair. His two partners, Jimmy and I, were not going to recommend it. Which we didn't. Bruce at that time was so desperate to become a star and believed so much in **The Silent Flute** that he felt to hell with the locations, we'll make it work. His attitude was it will work, it **will** work. I mean that was his attitude, 'Let's go guys, let's do it. We've got a hot company, they want to do it, why don't we do it?' Jimmy and I said no, and the result was that, very shortly after that, Bruce got an offer from Hong Kong to make a little picture called **The Big Boss**. He had now gone a month or two of having no money, and as Linda will tell you, they were truly strapped. I offered, and Coburn offered, to help financially. Bruce was insulted, because you know Chinese don't take charity. Bruce was too proud, and I don't know if Jimmy Coburn would admit it or not, there was also a stiffening in the relationship as a result of the failure of our trip. Especially when your livelihood is at stake, your career, your dreams.

"Then the offer came from Raymond Chow at Golden Harvest Studios. The terms were very very modest, I mean like a one-way ticket. So we said to Bruce, look, don't go unless you get the following: $25,000 a film and first-class round-trip tickets, because what will happen is you'll get over there, and I don't have to tell you about these Chinese guys, Bruce, and you're going to get over there, and you're not going to get your money and no return ticket and you're not going to be able to get home. You're stuck and your family is here. Get a round-trip ticket. We really tried to discourage him from going. He said no, he trusted this man. So he went and became a successful and famous star. Which shows you how much we know."

The Silent Flute, later renamed **Circle**

of Iron, was finally produced a few years later in 1978, and ironically starred David Carradine, the same actor who wrestled "Kung Fu" from Bruce years earlier.

Bruce was now being drawn into events that can be traced directly to an unlikely source, "The Green Hornet." Every scheme and plot failed, but the foreign television sales of "The Green Hornet," most particularly in Hong Kong, were forging an audience of television viewers who were proud of their Chinese countryman. The growing block of fans were, in turn, triggering interest from the press, and through them, interest from Raymond Chow, Run Run Shaw and other independent producers. Bruce was not struggling in a vacuum, though he could have no idea of what was stirring, however slow the buildup.

Chapter Eight

Golden Harvest

Raymond Chow's Golden Harvest Studios had been living on the edge ever since he started his own company. Shaw Brothers was the colossus of Asia with enormous distribution and hundreds of its own theaters. Along with this, Shaw Brothers was a studio the size and equal of MGM in that studio's great days. There were no antitrust laws in Hong Kong to prevent a monopoly of this sort. Raymond, for years, was Run Run's top man at the Shaw studios. There was a falling out between the two over several issues, many of which have yet to be satisfactorily explained. Yet, one story is known. Sir Run Run had taken as a concubine a singer in Hong Kong named Mona Fong. Sir Run Run then gave her the position of manager in charge of general affairs and she quickly maneuvered for a position over Raymond Chow. This may well have convinced Raymond to leave Shaw Brothers, aware of the old maxim, "Never challenge the bed." He secured enough financing to get off the ground, but he was making cheap pictures, even by cheap Hong Kong standards, and they were not breaking records. It was a very lean time for Chow and his partner Leonard Ho, and few thought Golden Harvest would survive. Shaw Brothers was in a position to squeeze them and deny screens for their product. In those

"I am going
to be the biggest
Chinese star
in the world."

days, Golden Harvest Studios was a primitive cluster of two rotting sound stages and a few outbuildings that held support facilities. It was set among squatters' shacks and perched rather precariously on a Kowloon hillside. Hong Kong hillsides are notorious for sliding and burying people during typhoons. Golden Harvest's financial situation was even more precarious than the hillside location of its studio. But far off in the United States, there was a fellow Chinese, a fellow countryman, who would turn all this around and smite Sir Run Run as well.

Raymond sent the wife of his director, Lo Wei, whose name is Liu Liang Hwa, to get Bruce's name on a contract. She was considered a hard-nosed negotiator. She went to Los Angeles to do Raymond's bidding, stating her boss's position and stabbing a finger at Bruce. "But Bruce didn't have any trouble with her," Linda said. "He was rather **charming** himself."

About this time, Fred Weintraub, who had been pushing for Bruce to star in the "Kung Fu" series, heard from Bruce. Fred said, "I got a call from Bruce, who said he was going to make two pictures for Raymond Chow. I told him to send me a print of the first picture and maybe we could revive a project at Warners. Six months later I got a print of **The Big Boss**. It started to get people charged up again. Then, several months later, a copy of **Fist of Fury** arrived. I knew he had something going. Raymond then offered me the American rights to those two pictures for $25,000. I didn't have the $25,000 at that moment and couldn't raise it in time. Those two pictures eventually grossed between $15 and $20 million."

Summer in Thailand is very much like most of Southeast Asia—miserable. Humidity soars along with the heat, and insects prey on the unwary. It is not as bad in the capital

Dan Inosanto (left in photo) was among Bruce Lee's best students and closest friends. Inosanto was charged with carrying on the precepts of jeet kune do after Bruce's death in 1973.

In a scene from the movie, *The Big Boss*, Bruce Lee leaps over a flying dog. *The Big Boss*, also known as *Fists of Fury*, broke all Asian film box-office records by grossing $3.2 million.

city of Bangkok, where air-conditioned restaurants and hotels can be found, but Bruce was not to linger there, being whisked through Bangkok and north to the small town of Pak Chong. Conditions, then and now, are primitive at best, especially for someone who had left his home in sheltered Los Angeles.

The one small hotel in the village provided miserable accommodations. The bath water ran yellow and mosquitos ran wild. While they ate, flying insects would drop into their bowls of rice. They would pick them out and then eat quickly before more collected. Through all of this, Bruce said nothing. He simply wanted to get it done and gone.

Bruce was determined to ignore the weather, poor food, lack of proper sanitation, and isolation from any form of communication except an erratic postal service. He was making movies, that was enough. He suppressed his impatience with crude equipment and a script that gave very little clue to the story. He held himself in check in the first five days while the director of the film, Wu Chai-Wsiang, whose violent temper was a matter of public knowledge, shouted and screamed at cast and crew until the production manager, the same woman who had signed Bruce to a contract, Liu Liang Hwa, could take no more. She returned to Bangkok and called Raymond Chow to have Wu replaced. The studio did not staff directors but Raymond knew that Liu's husband, Lo Wei, was to finish a picture in Taiwan and would be flying to Hong Kong in a couple of days. Lo was dispatched to Thailand to meet Bruce, a relationship that would finally end in threats of death.

In her book about Bruce, Linda quoted a letter she got from Bruce that said, in part, "The film I'm doing is quite amateurlike. A new director has replaced the old one. This new director is another so-so one with an almost unbearable air of superiority."

Lo Wei said, "I shot **Big Boss** with three scraps of paper." Meaning that he had no script to work with and only meager ideas on which to base the story. "One day," Lo says, "we were shooting in an ice house and Bruce started yelling, 'Aiya! Disaster! Disaster!' We all stopped because we didn't know what was disastrous and he said he dropped his eye glasses. I told him he didn't wear eye glasses. But then he said it was his contact lens. So everybody didn't dare move a step, afraid to break it. Everybody at the ice house, dozens of people, bent down to look for it. Not easy with tons of ice and thousands of ice chips. We trained the lights on the floor and it was an hour before it was found. Bruce found it himself. I wonder if he didn't do that on purpose just to disrupt things. Maybe he had the lens in his pocket all the time, eh?"

Bruce was losing weight and having trouble eating something that would stay down. He was eating canned meat because there was little in the way of fresh, or frozen, beef and chicken, and he was not sure he could trust it when some was found. There was none of his beloved barbecued pork. The debilitating days dragged on and after only two weeks he felt that he had been there "a year."

Bruce said, "We used all existing locations. Even the whorehouse was real and it was very dirty and it stunk. And the poor prostitutes were very ugly. They got 15 patts a trick, which is about 75 cents, and the production company paid them 200 patts not to do anything and keep out of the way."

He was plagued with an assortment of afflictions. His back, aggravated by the fights, was giving him trouble, he turned an ankle during another piece of action, and then cut his hand, which would again happen in the making of **Enter the Dragon** and lead to a vendetta with another martial artist. Lo Wei said, "He was always taking a lot of medicine. I remember at that time I had trouble with my gallbladder and I went to see a doctor. I said I had pain in the nervous system of my back. I thought it was the

Lo Wei (center) and Bruce Lee had a running feud after working together on *The Big Boss*. Bruce claimed Lo Wei had no knowledge of how to shoot martial arts action while Lo Wei took credit for making Bruce a star.

Asian audiences got their first glimpse of the famous Bruce Lee pose – fists clenched, muscles tight, eyes riveted on the target – in *The Big Boss*, which made him an overnight sensation.

nervous system's pain. I was ignorant. Actually I had gallstones. Bruce saw the doctor give me an injection and he wanted an injection, too. He said he had a pain in the back from an injury and so the doctor gave him an injection like mine. He always wanted to use other people's medicine."

Bruce and Lo had similar temperaments. Both were prideful men with short tempers, but Bruce had the added facility of swearing with great gusto, ingenuity and vulgarity. Lo had an aversion to swearing and his face would pinch with the sound of a bad word. Lo thought Bruce was swearing at him. Bruce said, "I'm swearing at my father." Lo said, "Swearing at your father. He is dead six years. So I wondered about this Bruce Lee. I could not understand him."

Toward the end of the picture, Raymond Chow flew in from Hong Kong to meet his new employee. To that day he had only talked to Bruce by phone several times. Their relationship would last only three years, but the chemistry of their partnership would reshape and revitalize the Hong Kong film industry. Bruce is quoted in Linda Lee's book as telling Raymond that he "was going to be the biggest Chinese star in the world."

Some of the world's finest stuntmen are the Chinese working out of Hong Kong and several were sent to Thailand to work with Bruce on the picture. When they returned they praised this new man to everyone and called him, "Lee sum geok,' or 'Lee three legs." It meant Bruce was so lightning fast it seemed he had three legs. The stuntmen never lost their respect or admiration for Bruce. They were always there to help or protect him. And when **The Big Boss** opened in Hong Kong a few months later, he fulfilled his "star" prophesy. Chinese superstar Jackie Chan has made pictures that have eclipsed Bruce's Hong Kong grosses, as have others in this day of higher ticket prices, but none has come close to his standard set on an international level. Bruce's ultimate aim was achieved after his death, acclaim flowing

Before the premiere of *The Big Boss*, Bruce Lee predicted his star would rise higher than any in Asian film history. Many scoffed at the words, but when the film opened to huge audiences, his prophesy turned out to be true.

101

in from every corner of the world. He was never interested in being crowned "King of Hong Kong," as the press called him. His eye was on much more than local, or even Asian, recognition. His view was global from the very beginning.

The Big Boss was an instant sensation in the Far East. The Chinese started a life-long love affair with Bruce that failed to abate with his death. He did more for the Chinese psyche than any dozen politicians and martyrs. This acted as gut-level therapy for millions of overworked and underprivileged people, who may tell you they are the ultimate and superior race, but in reality suffer from self-doubt and inferiority. Bruce rekindled a feeling of pride and literally brought his countrymen to their feet screaming and cheering in hundreds of theaters. They suddenly felt better about themselves and could take another day with a little less pain and prejudice. This accomplishment alone is enough to set Bruce forever in the collective awareness of those he touched. Minorities the world over, who to this day do not believe he died but has simply stepped away a moment to refresh himself and to return at the proper moment, view Bruce as their representative and spokesman.

Lo Wei publicized himself as the "first Chinese million-dollar director." Lo was a devout gambler with a special liking for the horse races at Happy Valley Race Track. At times with the radio thundering on the set, he would ignore the actors who were trying to play out a scene. This could be done because sync sound was not used during a "take," with the voices being dubbed later on a sound stage. Still, Bruce was enraged by his lack of interest in the film. With all his excesses, Bruce never was accused of turning his back on a film or not trying to do his best.

While making **The Big Boss**, "Longstreet" aired in the United States. It was the opening show of the fall season of 1968 and got a great deal of acclaim, largely credited

Here are two shots from *The Big Boss*. Despite the success of the film, Bruce Lee's relations with director Lo Wei could only be called "strained." Bruce did not like Lo Wei, nor did he respect him. Plus, after the film was released, Lo Wei said he was the real "star" of the picture. This would later lead to a confrontation between the two.

to Bruce's appearance. The critics were nearly unanimous in praising Bruce as an actor as well as a martial artist. It was the best thing Bruce had done up to then and Paramount Studios immediately set about tracking him down through Hong Kong and then the remote location in Thailand. They sent numerous telegrams, enhancing Bruce's reputation and worth in the eyes of the location company and Golden Harvest executives in Hong Kong. Paramount offered him three more shows with a payment of $1,000 a show, with his appearance being limited to three days for each show. With a contract for another Golden Harvest picture in his pocket, Bruce asked for double the money. They agreed. When **The Big Boss** "wrapped" he flew back to Los Angeles and his family, and then to Paramount to meet the "Longstreet" obligations. The later shows did not turn out as well because the initial offering was written especially for Bruce by Silliphant, whereas he was rather hurriedly inserted into the plots of the following shows. The show and Bruce's performance suffered from the haste. Still, he was a little richer and freer. Before returning to Hong Kong for the second Golden Harvest picture, **Fist of Fury**, he and Linda sold the home that had caused so much strain on their budget and made a $10,000 profit on the transaction. Bruce had several television offers at this time, which he thought he would accept once the second feature was finished. He never envisioned himself staying in Hong Kong for any length of time, not even as success followed success. Even after **Enter the Dragon** he planned to relocate in the United States.

Bruce now packed up his family and they left for Hong Kong and Bruce's next Golden Harvest film, arriving in October for the premiere of **The Big Boss**. The word on the film was out and they were met at Kai Tak Airport by thousands of people and heavy press coverage. The great love affair between Bruce and the Chinese public was launched. A large group of Boy Scouts paraded with their brass band and the Golden Harvest publicists were beating drums of their own. Great! Fantastic! Not to be believed! And the picture supported their wildest claims. It was an explosion in Hong Kong and other cities in Asia. Until Bruce's next picture, it became the highest grossing film of all time in Hong Kong, surpassing **Gone with the Wind**, **The Sound of Music**, and **The Godfather**. It revolutionized the film business in Hong Kong, and gave actors a bigger voice in dealings with the studios. The Chinese had found a new hero and, miraculously, he was Chinese. Ticket prices rose as demand for seats far exceeded supply.

Bruce and Linda moved their young children into a flat on Waterloo Hill, 2 Man Wan Rd. and 13 flights up, one of the few numbers not considered unlucky to the Chinese. The flat was furnished and the studio paid the rent. Brandon was enrolled in La Salle College, the school from which Bruce had been expelled 14 years earlier.

At night they heard the loud clacking of the mahjong tiles as gamblers slammed them on the wooden tables in the neighborhood. There was an elevator which seldom worked. Climbing 13 floors was a chore until they made it an exercise by running the distance with the children in their arms. This was, in effect, Bruce's first exercise machine in Hong Kong. This apartment building was typical of the Hong Kong landscape: hundreds of bamboo poles jutting out from narrow balconies held the day's laundry. Linda tried placing a pole, heavy with wash, out to dry, but watched in horror as it fell 13 stories. "Luckily it managed to miss everybody."

Chapter Nine

"Where's Bruce?"

The American television proposals vanished from their minds when Linda and Bruce attended the premiere of **The Big Boss**, which occurred shortly after they arrived in Hong Kong in October, 1971. It was to be a late-night screening and the publicity people of Golden Harvest had done their job, jamming the theater to capacity. Most new films are premiered at midnight, usually for a charity such as the Boy Scouts. Bruce and Linda sat with the usual opening-night apprehensions, and the top executives of Golden Harvest, Raymond Chow and partner Leonard Ho, were there to view what destiny held for their company. Before the picture finished they knew a "new star had risen in the East." The audience could not find voice enough to express its approval. They yelled and screamed and left the theater to spread the word through the streets where motion pictures are really made. By daybreak Bruce Lee's name was being heard in restaurants, at bus stops and on ferries plying between Kowloon and Hong Kong Island. Film critics typed the good news, though they would insist on spelling his name in the Chinese manner, Li. He was one of their own and they did not intend to share even the spelling of his name with the West. When a Chinese audience dislikes a film, it has been known to cut the seats with knives.

"This guy's going to be it. He's a winner."

Marring the great moment of the release of his first major film was the death of James Lee, whom Bruce considered more of a father than his own father. It bothered Bruce that James had not seen the acclaim that was coming from the Asian public.

There was no threat with this movie.

Mel Tobias, Hong Kong film critic and film historian, tells of that night: "I didn't know who Bruce Lee was. It was just by accident that I saw the first show. I had a guest from Manila and he wanted to see a midnight show, and the midnight show was **The Big Boss**. When the film ended there was about ten seconds of silence. They didn't know what hit them, and then they started roaring, you know. Because it was the first exposure, it was a midnight show, you know, to get the public reaction. I always go to the midnight shows, because the midnight shows have all the essentials together, the audience response. And when they saw Bruce Lee, they were just completely stunned. And then the applause afterward, which was thunderous. And that feeling I had: This guy is going to be **it**. You **know** the way he projected the Oriental and the Asians gave us a sense of identity. Here was an Asian who had been squashed but reserved his energy, which is very Oriental. And in the last moment he would win. He's a winner. And for an Oriental, that is very important.

The audience was yelling, "Where's Bruce! Where's Bruce!" But the studio executives were hustling Bruce and Linda out to a waiting car.

Bruce and Linda had sent air tickets to James Lee in Oakland so that he could come to Hong Kong for the premiere, but they were informed that James had died a short while before. This took most of the enjoyment out of Bruce's triumph. James had not lived long enough to see the acclaim his friend and partner got that midnight in Hong Kong.

For now the press would only praise Bruce. He could do no wrong nor think dark thoughts. He had entered the honeymoon of his Saint Bruce period. Some, even today, will tenaciously protect his memory from attack from any quarter. Robert Chan remembers leaving the Astor Theater in Kow-

Bruce Lee spent much of his life seemingly fighting shadows. On one occasion, he was found in a room viewing a tape of former heavyweight champion Muhammad Ali and mirroring his moves. Bruce was convinced he someday would have to fight the great boxer.

loon to step out into a heavy downpour. Chan, speaking in broken English, said, "It was rain very heavy. Bruce Lee kindhearted. Man delivering cooked rice on stacked plates on bicycle, passing theater, fall suddenly, heavy, pouring rain, him and I with one umbrella. Both wear Western suit and tie. We would go to Nathan Restaurant to drink. Bruce run out to person where fall. Prove he is kindhearted. Doing think like this. Helped person put things back properly. Took $10 from pocket to give person. For person or to pay back his boss or customers. This proves this man."

Robert Chan also mentioned that Bruce had heard of a friend who was trying to kick a drug habit. Bruce traced the fellow to a decrepit old house on Cheung Lok Street off Jordan Road. Bruce tried to dissuade him from using drugs and talked him into seeking help at a rehabilitation center. Bruce also got a doctor for the man and bought him vitamins. The friend promised he would break his habit and Bruce kept buying the vitamins until he discovered the man was selling the tablets to pay for more drugs. Bruce was truly disappointed that he had failed to help his childhood pal. "This proves the man," Robert Chan reiterated.

Robert Elegant, in his book about Hong Kong, quotes a scholar of the Chinese culture, upon being asked what it was that Chinese like most: sex, gambling or food. The scholar pondered the question at length. "That's a difficult question," he said. "It's hard to say if it's gambling or food." Bruce probably would have agreed. He had a great love of food. He ate most anything and with gusto and animation. Linda talks about him sitting down to a meal of hot and spicy Korean food and sweating his way through dish after dish, gorging himself while drenched in perspiration. He had favorite foods, of course, and barbecued pork was high on the list. Robert Chan said that when Bruce's mother did not serve barbecued pork at home, he would often take to the streets to

find it. Pig intestines, orange-colored chicken claws and raw squid were three of his favorites as a boy and bird's-nest soup held a special fascination for him. Bird's-nest soup comes in several styles usually identified by color. For instance, there are red nests, gray nests and nests of a greenish color. These nests are created by sea swallows that occupy caves along the coast of the South China Sea. Beyond the obvious presence of bird droppings, the most common ingredient is swallow's saliva, which holds the small nest together. Now, the saliva is a derivative of what the swallow eats. They prefer seaweed, various fungi, seaworms, numerous flying insects and sap from several varieties of trees. These delicacies, and more, combine to produce a saliva of unusual and desirable taste and odor. Young boys are paid to climb into the caves and pluck the nests, much of the time against the wishes of the swallows. The nests are then cooked in boiling water to distill the essence of the flavor much like chicken soup.

Linda had only one real friend in Hong Kong, Rebecca Hui, an American of Japanese descent. Rebecca had just married a Chinese man, Sam Hui, who worked for Raymond Chow, and who later became a famous recording artist in Hong Kong. He established grosses for record sales that have never been equaled. The newlyweds were given one of Raymond's exotic dinners that included many dishes unfamiliar to Linda and Becky. "I remember," Linda said, "Becky and I glancing across the table and making the most ugly faces about the food. I'm sure it looked very rude, and now, of course, we eat it all and love it."

Before becoming enamored with Chinese cooking, Linda and Brandon would walk to the Mandarin Hotel for sausages, looking for something "Western" among all the home cooking. Another time, while searching for a place to eat, Linda was standing at an intersection with Rebecca, waiting for a light to change. Two Chinese women were stand-ing next to them and one said in loud Chinese, "Do you know who that woman is?" pointing at Linda. Her friend shook her head and the first woman said, "That is Bruce Lee's wife!" Linda turned to the woman and said in Chinese, "This is my Japanese friend from America. She doesn't speak Chinese, but as you can see, I do."

Bruce, now, was preparing for the second of his Golden Harvest pictures. Even though he expected problems with the next production, he was always looking "down the road."

One day Bruce was found at the studio screening a Muhammad Ali documentary. Ali was the World Heavyweight Champion at the time and Bruce saw him as the greatest fighter of them all. The documentary showed Ali in several of his fights. Bruce set up a wide, full-length mirror to reflect Ali's image from the screen. Bruce was looking into the mirror and moving along with Ali. Bruce's right hand followed Ali's right hand. Ali's left foot followed Bruce's left foot. Bruce was fighting in Ali's shoes. "Everybody says I must fight Ali some day," Bruce said, "I'm studying every move he makes. I'm getting to know how he thinks and moves."

Bruce knew he could never win a fight against Ali. "Look at my hand," he said. "That's a little Chinese hand. He'd kill me."

The first of many to suddenly notice Bruce's worth was, and, of course he had known it all the while, was Sir Run Run Shaw. His first offer to Bruce was for the paltry sum of $2,000 a picture, made two months earlier, but now he upped that by $248,000 and sent a signed contract across town for Bruce's approval. Bruce turned it down. Undaunted, Sir Run Run sent another check; this one was blank. It all came too late and plans were rushing ahead to begin work on the second of Bruce's commitments to Golden Harvest. **Fist of Fury** was a story that expanded what Bruce had been doing. There were political and social levels to the script that gave it greater weight and wider

The rewards of fame. Above, Bruce surveys a photograph of a Rolls Royce Corniche, which he planned to purchase after the finish of *Enter the Dragon*. He ordered the car but died before he could pick it up. At left, Golden Harvest's Raymond Chow (right) looks at a birthday cake for Bruce on the set of *Enter the Dragon*.

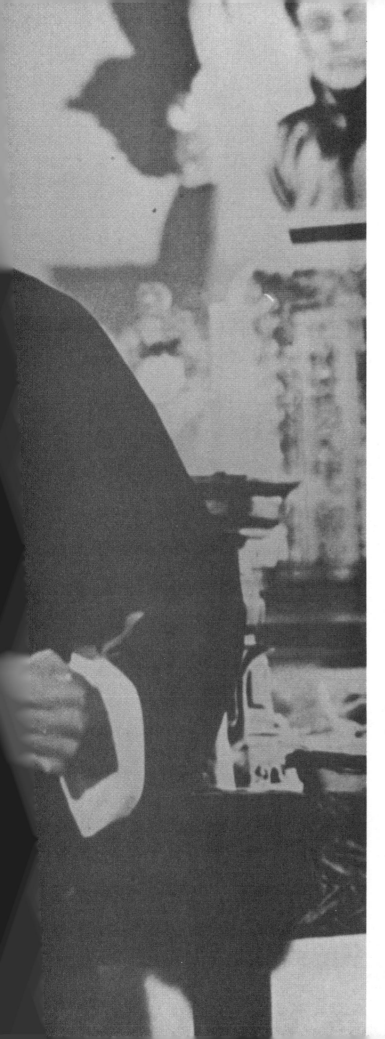

impact. The Japanese are not loved in China or Hong Kong and this was a story of Japanese subjugation and terror along with a new level of action and the perfection of Bruce's hair-raising yells and cries.

Still, **Fist of Fury** is a story so very common to Chinese films—a hymn to revenge. Its setting is well worked: a master's school and his students have been sullied and insulted. The action scenes are quite violent and prodigious amounts of "studio blood" darken the stage floor. His actions and attitudes come as close to a wild animal as they ever would and his "cry of doom" was in full voice. Veterans of the Korean conflict, who saw hundreds, and even thousands, of Chinese troops running headlong over a hill and screaming their blood-freezing battle cry, know how frightening this sort of tactic can be. Bruce made this kiai his own and all those who tried to emulate this chilling sound appeared quite foolish. It's a cry that could only come from him.

Bruce knew how deeply the hatred of the Japanese ran in his countrymen, though they might nod and half-smile while taking yen from Japanese tourists. All he needed was to light a match. One scene called for a huge thug, having just destroyed the Chinese students' school, to say, "The Chinese are the sick people of Asia." This line dug at the guts of the Chinese audience and it could not wait until Bruce dismantled the bastard. Near the end of the picture, when Bruce does just that, he turns to cast his malevolent gaze over the defeated Japanese and says, "The Chinese are **not** the sick people of Asia." The audience erupted into a frenzy that was frightening and then stood on the theater seats to howl its approval. Bruce had turned his audience into adoring slaves.

Bruce Lee, as shown in a scene from *Enter the Dragon*, his most successful film. In Bruce Lee, his Chinese countrymen saw a savior, a man who could instill a national pride that had been missing for generations.

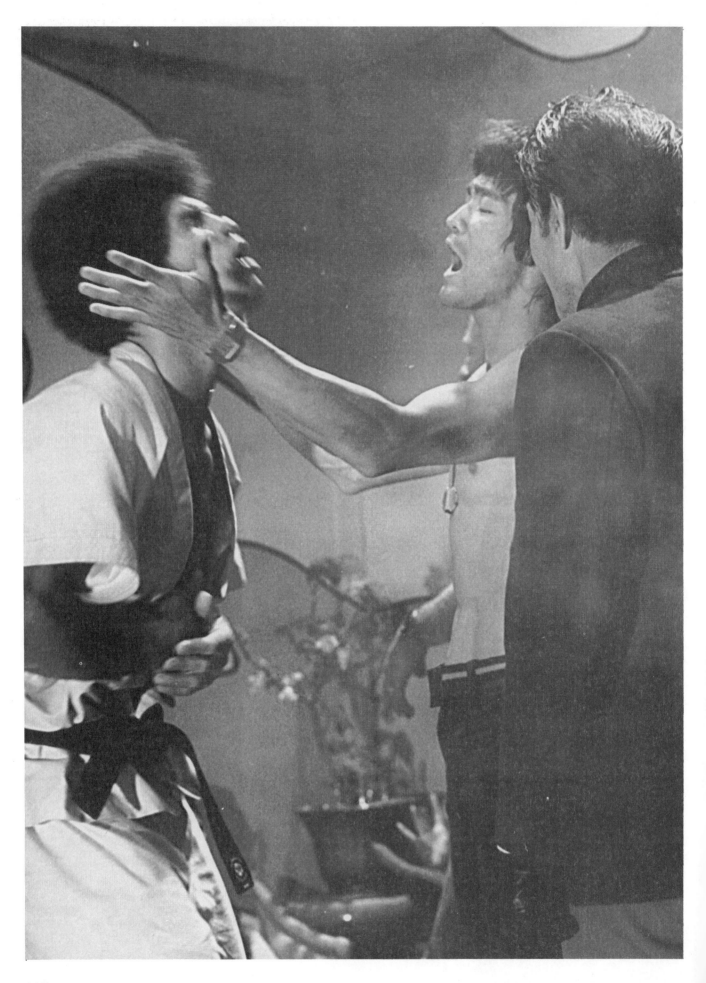

116

Chapter Ten

No Way, Lo Wei

Lo Wei had been signed to direct Bruce's second picture and their relationship, shaky as it was in Thailand, grew worse. The Chinese say, "River water does not go with well water." Toward the last half of the picture they could neither agree on any approach to the story nor on the way a character or scene should be handled. Bruce felt the stodginess and stubborness of his middle-aged director. Lo Wei says, "I don't have time to shoot loosely. I cannot tolerate. His face show he is very displeased. I saw that. I said, 'I know you are "red" (hot or popular) and I cannot say I made you so. It is your own ability. But even if you are red I have my pride.' I do not tolerate."

Again Bruce found there was no definitive script for **Fist of Fury**. In fact, he claimed there was hardly an outline. He wanted something fresh. Story plots rarely changed and sometimes only the costumes were new. "Warming over yesterday's rice," as the Chinese are apt to say. Even though this picture was to be shot on the studio lot, equipment and facilities were hardly better than they were in Thailand. Bruce was barely tolerating the man and he knew he could direct better by instinct than Lo could with all his experience. Lo had been an actor for a number of years and even played a part in **Fist of Fury**. He had directed at least 80

"River water does not go with well water."

pictures, most with Shaw Brothers before Chow hired him away.

Bruce found the production to be shoddily planned with little concept of what he had originally visualized. This alone does not insure a failed film. If a film's failure were to come about because the producers had little idea of what was going on, or that the script was being written at lunch, or that few got along with the director, or that the star was disgusted with the entire production, then **Casablanca** would never have become a classic.

Fist of Fury stumbled ahead as Bruce battled the oftentimes disinterested and inattentive Lo Wei. The director was a confirmed gambler who sometimes called it an early day so he could make the featured race at the track. Bruce silently boiled, and silence was not Bruce's strong suit. There were several clashes during the shoot and the Hong Kong press were quick to make them public.

They got through the picture, though a common animosity had been forged. This later would lead to murderous threats. Mercifully, the film finally wrapped and the footage was turned over to editorial.

Within two weeks of its opening, **Fist of Fury** had broken every record set by **The Big Boss** in Asia. The traffic jam in Singapore, brought about by the film, caused police to ask that the film be withdrawn for a week until they found a way to handle the overwhelming number of automobiles and people. And this was in the face of scalpers asking $45 for a $2 ticket.

Fist of Fury ran for eight months in the Philippines and drew such huge crowds that the government had the film taken from theaters for a few weeks to allow domestic fare a chance to make money. The response to Lee's movie was overwhelming.

Pictures of Bruce appeared daily in most Hong Kong newspapers. In a confined and congested area the size of Hong Kong, a celebrity of Bruce's magnitude took his life

Armed with new confidence after the success of *The Big Boss*, Bruce struck a deal with Golden Harvest's Raymond Chow to gain more control over what the studio produced. The eventual product of those discussions was Concord Productions.

into his own hands on the street. There was nowhere to hide outside the home. When Bruce walked down the street, a mob would quickly grow like the tail of a comet. Suddenly there were thousands following him. There were "blood-letting" fights on the street when pressing crowds tried to get Bruce's autograph. Bruce was amazed, and sometimes fearful for the safety of both fans and himself when he witnessed this raw, unleashed emotion.

Yet, he also understood the dark side of human nature because he knew his explosive temperament often blinded him and caused incidents he immediately regretted. He would get Linda to make a phone call or visit a person he offended to smooth out the "misunderstanding." Bruce could not make a call of that kind, being an excessively prideful man, though he would be genuinely contrite.

Robert Lee said, "Sometimes he got in a bad temper. And when I say bad, I mean **bad**. He's not the kind of person who cares who's around." Bruce once said to Linda, "I'm difficult to live with, aren't I?" He knew.

Though hardly an American was aware of it, a little Chinese fella in Hong Kong had become the world's foremost film property on the strength of his second picture. He exploded on the world's capitals and he would not slow down, even in death.

There also was a handful of motion picture executives in Hollywood who were following the figures out of foreign cities such as Buenos Aires, Rome and Singapore. The daily and weekly tallies of **Fist of Fury** came under watchful eyes. In Hong Kong itself, Run Run Shaw gazed gloomily at the figures, shrugged and remarked to a writer, "How could I know?"

Following closely behind the enormous success of the first two films, Lo Wei came back into the picture, seemingly with the agreement of Raymond Chow. Bruce understood film as well as Lo Wei and he understood the position he now had with the studio. In reality, he had saved the place.

And he would no longer work for wages. The next picture, **Stern Faced Tiger**, was being planned and Raymond went to Bruce with the proposal of having Lo Wei direct, but Bruce was adamant. He made it public he did not want Lo as a director again.

Then Lo Wei claimed, publicly, that Bruce did not understand fighting "for the camera." Lo said he was a good "street-fighter," but not accomplished in the ways of film. He told of teaching Bruce how to fight on the set of **The Big Boss**, a claim that is hard to accept. If Bruce was two things they were fight-wise and film-wise. Lo Wei had never been anything but head honcho and he was telling the press he was responsible for the success of the Bruce Lee films and that he had become Hong Kong's first "million-aire director." Bruce was livid and he smoldered as few can smolder. Bruce was not going to let Lo anywhere near his next production, though Golden Harvest execu-tives assumed that Lo would direct the next picture, ignoring what Bruce had been quoted as saying. As Linda put it, "No way, Lo Wei."

Bruce decided he was no longer going to be "the hired hand" at Golden Harvest and he went to see Raymond about that. Linda said, "Bruce saw Raymond and told him to move over. That they were partners." Bruce's initial contract had been fulfilled and Bruce was free to consider other offers, which he could have done at great profit. Chow certainly did not want Bruce wandering down the road to Run Run's establishment, or anywhere else. They formed a company as equal partners and separate from Golden Harvest called Concord.

Yet, even with this new agreement, Raymond told Lo Wei to get a script ready for production called **Stern Faced Tiger**, starring Bruce. The picture was to be shot in Japan starting Jan. 6, 1972. Lo Wei, whose statement is the only one I have to go by, said the production was ready to go when he got a call from Raymond Chow telling him

Through his films, Bruce Lee introduced a new set of weapons to the action audience. One of those weapons, the nunchaku, skyrocketed in popularity after it was featured in *Enter the Dragon*.

that Bruce no longer wanted to do **Stern Faced Tiger**. Raymond had said, "It seems he doesn't want to shoot." Lo Wei said, in his half-learned English, "What this? He making fun with us." Lo called Bruce and met him at the Kui Fu Ren restaurant. Lo said, "How about it? We are ready to go, visas been issued." Then Bruce told him the script was not very good. Lo wanted to know where Bruce felt the script was weak. Lo said, "If **you** shoot a film that is no good and fail you can go back to America and teach kung-fu. If **I** shoot a picture that fail, I cannot work anymore. Would you not say I would be more careful than you? The script is prepared. I recognize it is very good. I am at ease." Bruce said he still thought the story was bad. Lo claims he told Bruce, "Then tell me where it is no good and I will change. You are big star, you change to your satisfaction. I will have to agree to it." Bruce said he could not spell it out. Lo Wei went on, "Do not say you cannot spell it out. Is it scene number three, or number five? Number seven? Number eight? Which scene dialogue wrong, story development wrong? Must be reason. You just cannot say no good, but **where** no good." Bruce said he would go home and think about it and write Lo the next day. Lo contends he told Bruce to take more time, maybe three days. Bruce said he would and Lo felt Bruce left in a happy mood. Then 16 days passed and Lo had not gotten a letter from Bruce, nor had he called. Lo decided that the situation had deteriorated. He had also heard, round about, that Bruce wanted to direct his next film. Lo said, "If he was going to direct he will not be acting in my film. I decided that **Stern Faced Tiger** was dead. But Raymond said it must go ahead anyway since all preparations had been made in Japan. No choice. In that case we would have to replace Bruce. Raymond Chow got Jimmy Wang Yu, a very popular Chinese actor, to come back from Taiwan. He replaced Bruce with Wang Yu. The feud with Bruce was mainly caused by this change. Later, many things happened."

It's not true their "feud" began with this change of casting, though it certainly caused it to grow more bitter and violent. Here is Bruce with no intention of making the film, but not willing to accept being replaced by another actor. Their relationship, from the first week in Thailand and their first film together, was marked with distrust and hostility. Bruce considered Lo to be conceited and dictatorial, and above all, lacking in fresh and creative thought. Finally Bruce got Lo on the telephone, though I only have Lo's recollections of these confrontations. "Bruce asked me why I wanted to change my leading actor. I told him I did not receive any information from him. He promised three days and now it was one month that he phoned me the first time." Bruce countered with the "fact" that he had not said he did **not** want to shoot the picture. Lo replied it had been a month that he had taken to tell him this. Bruce had wanted to know why he wanted to change to Wang Yu and did Raymond Chow have anything to do with it? Was it Raymond's idea? Lo said, "You are a big star. I am a big director. I have my self-respect. You and I agree on three days. Nearly one month you ignore me. Very unsatisfactory." Bruce told him that by changing actors it made him look bad. Lo said that it did not make Bruce look bad. "I also know you are preparing your own film," Lo said. "Your own film will start pretty soon. I hear you want to direct. You are a big star. If you say at one o'clock that you want to be director, then they will be ready for you at three o'clock and you will be director at five o'clock." Bruce, growing more and more angry, as was Lo, told Lo that changing to Wang Yu showed how "di chang" he was, which is to say Lo used "underhanded tactics." Lo claims that Bruce cooled down a bit and said, "Let's do it. This way, I go with you and you don't change to Wang Yu. I'll come to shoot." Lo replied, "This is not good. Because you ignored me one month I change to others. I cannot change again. Otherwise how could I stand up as a man?" Lo says that Bruce got extremely angry and began to "swear towards me." Lo said he admonished Bruce for using language like that, his being a top star, and that Bruce swore at him again and hung up. They avoided one another after that, turning away when they would meet at the studio. The situation eventually came to a head at Golden Harvest. Why Bruce went through all this, having already made a deal with Raymond Chow to form another company to do a different picture, and then saying he **would** do **Stern Faced Tiger**, is incongruous.

So Bruce and Raymond Chow created Concord Productions. They were equal partners, with Bruce on the creative side and Chow taking care of the day-to-day business decisions, though he was not supposed to take any major steps without informing Bruce. This later caused problems when Bruce accused Raymond of making deals and selling territories without a word being said. Bruce wanted to write his own scripts and direct them when he could, and, too, he wanted a bigger slice of the profits. He felt it was his presence in these films that was drawing the ever-growing grosses, which was true. This attitude was very new to Hong Kong. Players, no matter what their stature, got only what the studio wanted to give and not a Hong Kong dollar more; they were to keep their mouths shut and their reputations reasonably clean. No star had ever been a partner in a studio operation and Bruce was lifting all actors' fortunes as he lifted his own. The film people of Hong Kong, as well as the lesser technicians, owe a great deal to Bruce and his fight for better pay and conditions. Their positions were a little more bearable when Bruce demanded more for himself, and by example, for them. He wanted to raise the level of the product produced in the Far East and he knew this would be accomplished through greater incentives. Sometimes he would despair at

doing this alone and would tell Linda he was returning to the United States for good where the scripts were better and professionalism was a way of life.

Bruce also disagreed with the "style" of filming that remains prevalent in Hong Kong. A director might simultaneously be directing two or three films, and at different studios, back and forth, or working one place on Monday and another on Tuesday. The actors work the same way, simultaneously appearing in several productions and precariously juggling days and times of days. Some have been known to be acting in seven or eight films at one time.

No matter how much a film grossed, no one but the producers shared in the profits. The actors were paid a salary, and a poor one at that, and were not allowed participation. Bruce railed against this system and loudly demanded that the producers set aside a certain percentage of the profits for the artist involved, which in turn would have encouraged everyone to give a little more of himself and stimulate the industry.

Bruce did more to raise the level of competence, build confidence and bring Hong Kong films to international attention and recognition than anyone else. Professional expertise has reached higher levels and their approach to filmmaking has shed its inferiority. The cycle of "chang-tow," or fight films, moves as the market moves, to "jung-tow," or films aimed at those who prefer more sex. These cycles rise and fall with an audience that waxes and wanes, but, in any case, it is alive and Bruce is credited with this revitalization of a stagnant and moribund industry. Everyone in the Hong Kong film industry owes a deep debt of gratitude to Bruce Lee.

Bruce began to prepare a script he had decided to direct himself called **Enter the Dragon**, a title he later, and wisely, changed to **The Way of the Dragon**. Linda said, "He did this not because he thought he was the best writer, or the best director, but because

he had no confidence in anyone in Hong Kong. So he sat down and had meetings and meetings and meetings with people at the studio and he started to write the script. To have a script ready before you started shooting was unheard of. This was a big breakthrough. The picture was made strictly for a Hong Kong audience. Very simple. It would not seem funny to us, but it went over very, very well in Asia. He knew the exact ingredients for the local people. It came from a whole knowledge of the Chinese tradition and culture."

This picture, principally shot in Rome, was probably the least of all Lee pictures and did very little business outside Asia. It was a very indulgent effort and the humor was dull and endless to the foreign eye, but it did show filmmakers in Hong Kong they did not have to be confined to their own locale. Again, Bruce was breaking from tradition and was casting his eye around the world. This, too, had never been done before. The film featured Chuck Norris in his first role and Nora Miao, a lovely Chinese actress who later would be romantically tied to Bruce.

Bruce used Caucasians for the first time. Norris had been one of Lee's exceptional students in Los Angeles and Bruce understood Norris' style of fighting. One of the problems in Hong Kong was finding good opponents who were big and quick. "You can't keep fighting midgets," Bruce would say. Chinese could double for Japanese, but they could not very well double for Caucasian villains.

Bruce's small company of filmmakers snuck around the streets of Rome, stealing locations and shots. They even arranged, illegally, to shoot much of the climactic fight in the Colosseum. The Italian authorities have not, for some time, allowed film companies on the premises and it had to be done as quickly and carefully as possible. An Italian film veteran guided them through. They finished the colosseum battle between Bruce and Chuck in Hong Kong by building a set that rather unfaithfully duplicated a portion of the great arena. Norris and some of the other Americans stayed in Hong Kong for a couple of months after the picture was finished. "They stayed just to have a good time," Linda said, "and it was nice to have some of our own kind around for awhile."

Bruce's brother, Peter, wanted to know all about the trip, but all Bruce wanted to talk about was the handmade, silk suits he had gotten in Rome. He was still the dandy that Linda first saw at Garfield High School.

Bruce had publicly predicted that **The Way of The Dragon** would make more money than either of his first two record-setting efforts and the press scoffed. He even said, quite confidently, the new film would gross over $5 million in Hong Kong alone, and again the reporters laughed. They could only shake their heads in disbelief when the film opened and brought in $5.4 million in its first run. They marveled at the accomplishment, but many were annoyed with what they saw to be a growing arrogance. The press was no longer his ally, rapturous in praise; instead, it began probing for weaknesses.

Bruce pointed out the film had cost more than most Hong Kong productions, but that his partner, Raymond, had sold the Taiwan rights for more than the entire budget. And he told them he would soon launch his next project, **The Game of Death**. All this the press dutifully chronicled, but its thoughts were beginning to stray toward more sensational aspects of his life. Who was he sleeping with? Surely he was not faithful to this pale gwie-lo girl. What was hidden and where? The writers would find out, and if they did not, they would **create** a secret life for Bruce.

A visiting reporter from Singapore, attending a function where Linda was present, went up to her and said, "It is said that Bruce is very close to certain actresses. How do you feel about it?" A witness said that Linda was momentarily stunned, then gallantly answered, "That is his matter."

Chapter Eleven

Bad Feng Shui

Bruce believed in fate and one's future foretold, but only to a degree. He treated the fortune-teller's thoughts at times with a certain disdain. "To hell with circumstances! I'll make my own circumstances!" he had told Linda. He felt he could change the hand that he had been dealt, yet he often spoke of a certain destiny that was compelling him to rush ahead and complete things as quickly as possible.

Bruce would not structure his life around the projections of a seer, but he did occasionally go to see fortune-tellers, especially in Hong Kong where thousands line the streets. They are a colorful lot, sitting on mats on the ground, or in booths near the many Buddhist temples. Some sit with their caged birds who help them determine a person's future. The fortune-teller fans out a couple dozen paper packets on the mat, and, in the light of a tall, glass-chimneyed alcohol lamp, lifts the tiny gate to allow the bird to pop out. The bird scrambles among the packets and snares one with its beak, handing it to his master. The bird promptly jumps back into the bamboo cage, having been fed a seed, and the seer opens the envelope to interpret the meaning of the message.

Bruce would sometimes seek out these people, hoping to confirm what he already

"To hell with circumstances! I'll make my own circumstances!"

The Game of Death brought Bruce Lee together with two of his closest friends and training partners: Kareem Abdul-Jabbar (top) and Dan Inosanto (above).

believed. He read his American horoscope, too, and he even sent away for computerized printout sheets that held vast amounts of information, suggestions and prognostications. They often ran to 20 pages.

And then there are the Feng Shui men. Belief in spirits and the supernatural is very strong among the Chinese and to be impudent can be very costly. The Feng Shui man is called in to determine quite a number of items, from where the children should be sent to school to the placement of a lamp in the living room. There must be a certain harmony of all spiritual and material things. He carries a large, circular device that resembles a box compass. Its magnetic needle is free to rotate on a horizontal dial, but the dial does not show directional points. Instead, it is marked with the 12 signs of the Chinese zodiac. If a home is to be built, the Feng Shui man will be asked which way it should face and possibly how many rooms it should have. The Feng Shui man who Bruce called in about the house he was going to buy in Kowloon Tong was not happy with the purchase. It had bad Feng Shui. One, it was under the flight approach to Kai Tak Airport, which would disturb the wind currents. Two, it was facing the wrong way, but nothing could be done about that. The Feng Shui man suggested a mirrored figure be placed on the rooftop to help with the inherent weaknesses in the building. The day before Bruce died, the figure was blown off the roof during a violent storm. It was this sort of happening that people point to when something dreadful occurs.

Mel Tobias, the Hong Kong film critic, said, "You know that Bruce Lee, in Chinese, means 'little dragon,' right? And that house he lived in in Kowloon Tong had something to do with dragons. Now, that area is ruled by nine dragons and I mean big dragons and they don't like little dragons. And you know that the **Chinese** are very superstitious. Well, this whole thing out there in Kowloon Tong smacks of bad Feng Shui. And you

Bruce thought of *The Game of Death* as the ultimate martial arts film. And it probably would have been had he lived to complete it. In this film he wore his now famous yellow track suit, still a staple in some martial arts studios.

never put the word **death** in the title of a book or play or movie. And then Bruce came up with this title **Game of Death**! Bad Feng Shui!"

Death in general, and the dead in particular, are more a part of the daily lives of Chinese than they are in Western cultures. Many festivals, such as "Sweeping of the Graves," observe the dear departed. During New Year's celebrations, people often buy several "simulations" of material items to send to dead relatives. Shops hold thousands of automobiles and television sets, air conditioners, refrigerators, etc., all made of tissue paper and papier-mache', which are burned in hopes the smoke will rise to the departed ancestors. These offerings are designed to give peace to the donor, and the recipient. The Lee family remembered many relatives in these rituals.

Another more direct contact with the deceased is a ritual called "Grandfather's Bones Jars," often called "Golden Pagodas." These earthenware jars, 30 inches high, are used to store the remains of one's parents or grandparents. Land is so scarce and expensive in Hong Kong, the price for a three-foot-by-six-foot plot can be $12,000 for just six years rent. At the end of the six-year tenure the bones will be dug up and sandpapered to a smooth luster. Then they will be interred in a large earthen jar and stacked with the feet at the bottom and skull at the top. Tens of thousands of these jars can be seen set on hillsides facing the sea. To purchase the same three-by-six space on a long-term basis can cost as much as $75,000.

Game of Death was to be the ultimate martial arts action film. Possibly, if Bruce had lived to complete it, it might have been something fine, though most of those who were close to the production felt it was being tossed together rather haphazardly. It was shot in segments whenever Bruce could arrange for a worthy foe to show up in Hong Kong, or in the case of Kareem Abdul-Jabbar, when someone happened to be in town on other business. Abdul-Jabbar had been one of Bruce's pupils in Los Angeles, and was visiting the Orient in 1972 for a vacation. Bruce thought it might be interesting to have a fight scene with someone over seven feet tall (Adbul-Jabbar stands 7-feet-2). The scene was eye-catching, if not strange, but it was not a memorable piece of action. Danny Inosanto was lured to Hong Kong for one sequence, and Bruce even asked his old friend, Taky, to fly from Seattle to appear in the film, but Taky declined, telling Bruce that he was no actor and he would only spoil it for him.

Chapter Twelve

Hollywood Calls

But before Bruce could complete **Game of Death**, he was interrupted by an offer from Warner Brothers and its two producers, Fred Weintraub and Paul Heller. Bruce was not unfamiliar to Weintraub. Fred had seen him at Hollywood parties and was involved in the concepts of the television series, "Kung Fu," though he dropped out before it went to pilot stage. Fred, too, believed Bruce was the obvious choice to play the lead in "Kung Fu" and was dumbstruck when it went to David Carradine. Bruce had written Weintraub at the outset of **The Big Boss**, describing what he was doing and Fred had asked him to send him a print of the completed film. When it was received, Fred ran it for Warners' executives and there was a good deal of interest, but nothing crystallized. Upon hearing that Bruce was about to start a second picture, Weintraub again asked to see a print. At that point, and with all the reports of theater grosses coming out of Hong Kong, along with box-office figures from scattered world markets, Warners began to focus on Bruce.

Game of Death was finished a few years after Bruce's death. Many millions of his worldwide fans waited anxiously for the film to be completed and rumors were widespread that the film contained the most electrifying hour of fight footage ever record-

"He appeared coming out of a 500-pound cake."

ed. Alas, this was not the case. Bruce left behind about 25 minutes of edited material, only 15 minutes of which was useable when a script was written to salvage it. Contrary to his own views on starting a project without a shooting script, Bruce had devised his ideas substantially on the set, with an overview of what he wanted to accomplish held fast in his head. The basic premise was known to several people, but a comprehensive concept could not be found.

Several people close to Raymond Chow suggested, and even pleaded, that the project be buried forever. But Raymond had the final, and compelling argument; the picture had been sold to the Japanese market, which paid a great deal for the privilege. The final cut, with an attempt to use two look-alikes, was disappointing at best. There were even some embarrassing moments such as the scene where a headshot, taken from a previous Lee film, was optically attached to the body of one of the doubles, the head turning strangely and eerily. Yet, the film was quite successful, as was most anything about Bruce Lee, no matter how tasteless or fraudulent. Imitators emerged in droves and sleazy films came forth with titles that used, Enter, Dragon, Fist, Connection, Game, Fury or Death in every possible combination. A dozen Bruce Li's strutted and screamed their way across the world's motion picture screens and many earned good money. The Bruce Li's were joined by Tarzen Lee, Tarzen Li, Bruce Le, Bruce Leong, Bruce Rhe, Kowloon Li, Rocky Lee, Jet Lee, Bronson Lee, Hong Kong Lee and Clint Lee. One actor even called himself Gypsy Lee. The number of film titles using Bruce's name would fill this page.

He found his name being used to promote products and films without his knowledge, and he was often quoted hyping pictures he had never seen. Everyone wanted

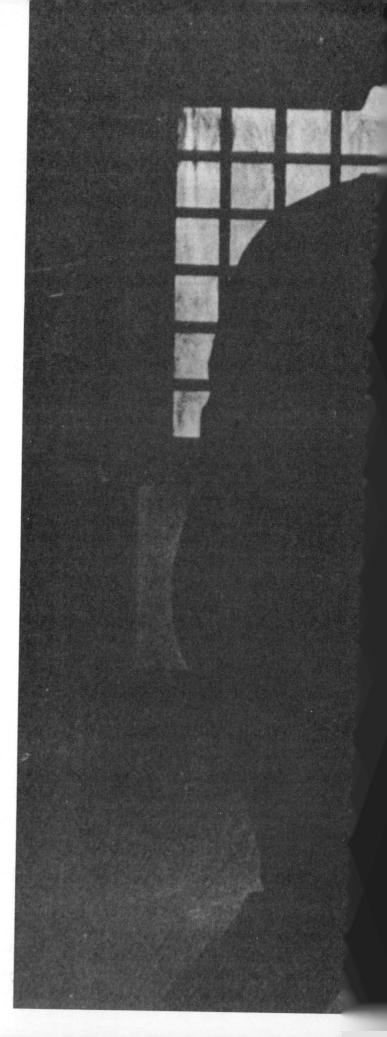

a piece of Bruce and he was feeling used by many and betrayed by some whom he had known for many years. His circle of friends grew smaller and tighter. His disdain grew along with an ever-present temper, and his patience dropped from its already low threshold.

"What I detest most is dishonest people who talk more than they are capable of doing," he once said. "I also find people obnoxious who use false humility as a means to cover their inadequacy. There is the other group of people who try to utilize me for their own ends. There was a producer who insisted that I go along to see the rushes of his new film. To oblige him I did. The next thing I knew advertisements for the film proclaimed in bold print that Bruce Lee had spoken highly of the picture."

Possibly the most disappointing act of this sort was brought about by Siu Kee Lun, or Unicorn, the young man who, with Pak Yan and Bruce, would go to the railroad station to knock down magnolia blossoms for an evening's entertainment and who worshipped Bruce in those early days. Pak Yan said Bruce had helped Unicorn financially after Bruce had gone to America. "Bruce," she said, "was very much concerned about Unicorn because Unicorn's family situation was not good. Financially Bruce helped him." Embittered by the success Bruce had gained, Unicorn betrayed him. Unicorn asked Bruce to help him with the fight choreography on a very low budget film in which he was starring called **Fists of Unicorn**. He prevailed upon Bruce to come to a location where a large fight scene was to be staged. Unknown to Bruce, the film's producers, and with Unicorn's connivance, had positioned a hidden camera so the action was recorded on film. The action with Bruce was used in the film, with notices proclaiming his large role. Bruce was angered and saddened about being used by Unicorn in this devious manner and they saw little of each other after that incident.

Unicorn died in a car crash in Malaysia during the summer of 1987.

Bruce was the featured guest on the "Enjoy Yourself Tonight" program that was celebrating the fifth anniversary of the Hong Kong Television Corporation. He appeared by "coming out of a 500-pound cake." It was never explained how this was accomplished, but, in any event, he appeared and was quickly surrounded by numerous film and television personalities. Among them was a famous heavyset actress by the name of "Fei Fei" (fat) Sham Din Ha. Also making a gushing appearance was Cantonese singer Cheng Kam Cheong, who came up close to face Bruce and began singing a song written especially for him called "Big Boss." The song's lyrics were so coyly flattering that people were getting uneasy with the syrupy thoughts. One viewer said, "It was vulgar and coarse and made people creep." Embarrassed, Bruce stood frozen in front of the singer, rubbing his nose and wondering what he should do or say. The master of ceremonies spoke of everyone being so "fond" of Bruce, which was apparently a gross understatement.

Fred Weintraub remembered, "I left for Hong Kong to set the final deal with Raymond. I was there for two weeks, but couldn't get Raymond to sign his name. He kept saying he thought it was a bad move for Bruce's career. Actually everyone figured it was a bad move for Golden Harvest since the studio might lose control of Bruce. Raymond was also making the deal so onerous that a deal was impossible. When I talked to Bruce he told me he was in favor of the project, but I could never get them in one room at the same time.

"Then, all of a sudden, it was the last night before I was to return to the States," Fred continued. "There was going to be a dinner party that night and I decided to give it a last shot. I even rehearsed exactly what I was going to say. Bruce took us to a Japanese restaurant he liked. We were

Although *The Game of Death* was financially successful, as were all Bruce's movies, most critics consider it his worst effort. Only a small amount of action footage depicting Lee was shot before his death, with much of it featuring Kareem Abdul-Jabbar and Dan Inosanto.

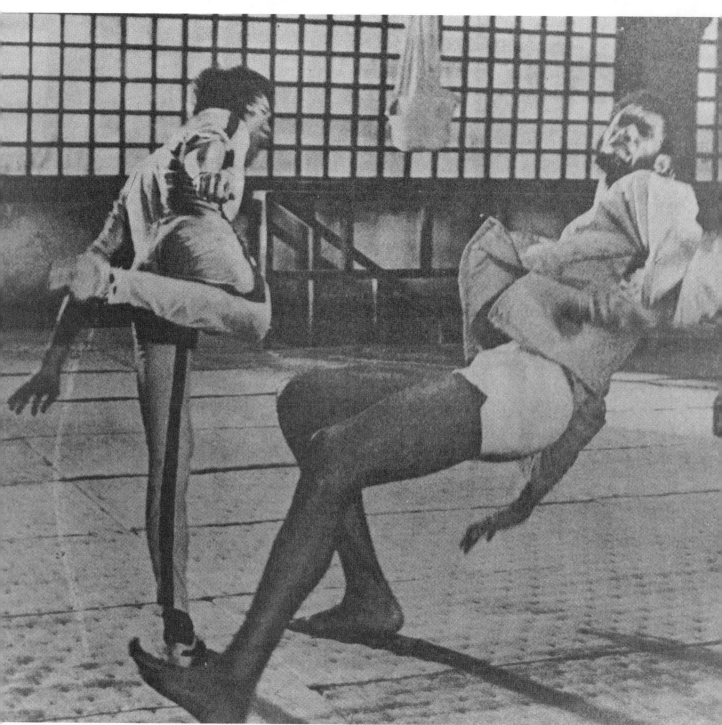

Kareem Abdul-Jabbar, who studied with Lee in the late 1960s, was added to _The Game of Death_ cast simply because he was in Hong Kong on vacation at the time of the shooting. Bruce's longtime friend, Taky Kimura, also was asked to be in the movie. He declined, however, citing a lack of acting experience.

instantly mobbed when we got out of the car. After dinner I told Bruce it was a shame, but probably true he'd never be an international star. I said Raymond was probably right and trying to go international might hurt his career rather than help it. Bruce wanted to know why it wouldn't work. I told him with the success of his career in Hong Kong it wasn't worth the gamble. With Raymond sitting nearby, I told Bruce I couldn't make a deal with Raymond, anyway. Bruce looked at me, then at his wife, Linda, and finally at Raymond. 'Make the deal,' he said. Raymond smiled and said, 'I think it's a wonderful idea.' I must admit, once Raymond was pushed into the deal, he was very supportive the rest of the way."

Bruce and Raymond Chow went to the United States to finish their Concord deal with Warner Brothers and the producers, Fred Weintraub and Paul Heller. They also set several actors and the director, who should, I believe, identify himself at this point. I am Robert Clouse, the author of this book. Now, from time to time, since I had become a part of the Bruce Lee saga as director of **Enter the Dragon**, I will relate certain incidents in the first person, periodically abandoning the exclusive use of the third-person format of this book.

Raymond and Bruce were staying at the Beverly Wilshire Hotel and one of the first things Bruce had to do was call Steve McQueen to tell him that he was back from Hong Kong and that he had become a successful actor. Bruce gloated about how his movies were doing big business and he was going to make a picture for Warner Brothers.

He really rubbed it in. McQueen said, "That's great, Bruce." The next day Bruce received an 8x10 glossy photograph autographed by McQueen: "To Bruce Lee, my greatest fan. Steve McQueen." It drove Bruce up the wall.

Lalo Schifrin, the composer of the **Enter the Dragon** music score, had been told to expect Bruce's "calling card" when they first met. Schifrin didn't believe it. Then, in the Warner Brothers executive dining room, Bruce shook Lalo's hand and stepped back to deliver his traditional greeting, a sudden kick toward Lalo's head which grazed his nose. Lalo felt only a breeze as Bruce's shoe passed by, and the speed of the kick gave Lalo no time to react.

Silent Flute came back into focus at this time when Bruce, still in Los Angeles, called Stirling Silliphant to say hello. He learned that Silliphant, in concluding a film deal at Twentieth Century Fox studios, arranged to have the making of **Silent Flute** included in the package. Silliphant remembers the conversation rather ruefully, believing Bruce would be happy and pleased that the long sought-after project had finally found a home. Instead, to Silliphant's amazement Bruce said, "I don't think you can afford me anymore. And why should I carry Coburn on my shoulders?" There was no doubt that Bruce still held a bitterness toward the treatment he received during the trip to India. Later, during the making of **Enter the Dragon**, he said, "If **Silent Flute** is ever made, Coburn will have to accept second-billing."

Chapter Thirteen

Bruce Explodes

Bruce and Raymond returned to Hong Kong and the American contingent left soon after. One of the Americans was the script's writer, Michael Allin, soon to be embroiled in a fight with the star over Bruce's concern with the dialogue. The fight eventually escalated into something more threatening.

Michael Allin did not get a lot of money for his script, but was offered a trip to Hong Kong in lieu of financial compensation. Many airline and hotel deals were available in those days. Bruce wanted to change several things in the script and decided to take advantage of Michael being on hand during filming. But they did not work well together.

Andre Morgan, a young man from Kansas who became Chow's most trusted and valued employee, said, "Bruce had some very specific requests in terms of what his Chinese character should say and the philosophy behind the application of kung-fu. Bruce took that very seriously, probably more than the rest of us. Michael made the mistake of being real smart alecky and talking back to Bruce. Bruce's attitude was, 'Hey, there's only one reason this movie's being made and that's because people believe that with Bruce Lee in the movie it's going to make back its negative cost. It's not being made because it's a fine piece of literature.'

"Enter the Dragon is not being made because it's a fine piece of literature."

"Bruce started out being really nice to Michael," Andre added. "He was being quite gracious to Michael, but it didn't work. Bruce had a fairly short fuse and it went very rapidly from 'Let's all work together on this,' to 'Get him out of here. I don't want to deal with him anymore.' Unfortunately, Michael had been promised a vacation in Hong Kong and was there to stay."

Several things happened next that seriously affected the film and Bruce's relationship with the producers. First, Fred Weintraub promised Bruce that Michael would leave Hong Kong the next day. Instead, Fred moved Michael to another hotel and told him not to make himself conspicuous. Then, in an interview with several reporters, Bruce told them of his unhappiness with Michael and how he told Allin to leave Hong Kong. He was going to leave, in fact, that very day.

To digress a moment: The Star Ferry Company runs ferries from Tsimshatsui in Kowloon across the harbor to Central in Hong Kong. Before the Japanese built a subway under the harbor, it was **the** way across the harbor for most people. There were eight ferries in service at peak periods and it cost six cents for first class and four cents for second class. Today it costs nine cents for first class. It's a beautiful trip and the greatest bargain in the world. In the '70s, 100,000 people made the trip each day.

Writer Robert Elegant, in his book about Hong Kong, tells of a ferry ride by an American tourist, who said, "Can you tell me where Chinatown is?" The attractive Chinese girl seated beside him smiled gently. "Don't move a single damned inch," she replied in the Indiana accent acquired from her American foster mother. "You're in it."

As fate would have it, Bruce's latest picture, **Fist of Fury**, had just opened and large posters had been installed in the ferry building in Kowloon and across the harbor in Hong Kong. Bruce decided to put on his sunglasses and view the new posters. Michael happened to take the same ferry across to Hong Kong. When Bruce came across Michael among the thousands and thousands of people who make that trip each day, he was dumbfounded, confused and ultimately very, very, angry. What if reporters came across this? Bruce suddenly realized he had been deceived and had misinformed the press.

This loss of face was cataclysmic. First, Bruce refused to continue shooting the film and then went about summoning up every Chinese curse he could against Fred and Paul. He went into a rage that lasted several days. When Paul or Fred came into a restaurant where Bruce was seated, Bruce got up and left. It took quite some time to smooth things out so everyone could work together again. But Bruce never totally forgave the producers.

Fred was becoming more and more impatient with Bruce and the delays he was causing. At one point he yelled he was going to fire Bruce and get another Chinese actor to play the part. "Who needs this guy?" he was heard to say. No one could take that seriously. Bruce was the reason the picture was being made.

Things were not going along as speedily as we had hoped. Plus, rumors and professional opinions began mounting in Hollywood and Hong Kong. They were saying there was no way a Chinese crew and an American crew could work closely together.

The production of **Enter the Dragon** got underway in January, 1973. Bruce was nervous, wary, even afraid about his first picture aimed at the international audience, and he doubted if this was the right vehicle. Expectations were very high. He delayed his arrival on the set several times and for several days. Other scenes were shot as the company worked around its reluctant star.

It was my belief (and Bruce's too), that he had to play to an international audience and not just to his adoring countrymen. To be an international star, he would have to look as much at home in New York or London as he

The two most famous fighting scenes in *Enter the Dragon* were against Bob Wall (top) and Shih Kien (left). Lee, who at one point early in the shooting wanted to cancel the picture, actually planned to kill Wall for injuring his hand. Order was restored by director Robert Clouse, who told Lee that Wall was needed for footage to be shot in the United States.

Considering all the troubles with shooting *Enter the Dragon*, it is a wonder the film ever got made. First, John Saxon (top left, watching Bruce slug Yeung Sze) thought he was the star of the film. Later, at the urging of revengful extras and stuntmen, Bruce was coaxed into thinking he had to kill Bob Wall to save face with his countrymen.

would in Hong Kong or Los Angeles. He could wear the beautiful silk Chinese suits with their flowing lines and wide cuffs, but he also would have to be carefully fitted in the best Western tailoring. And it paid off. In the cemetery scene where he went to his parent's graves to explain what he was about to do, he stood and bowed while dressed with impeccable taste. This type of attention to detail combined to form a mosaic of the new Bruce Lee. He was no longer the country bumpkin who ultimately outfoxes the city slickers. The Chinese audience did not like him as well as they had in his three earlier films, but the worldwide audience took to him with greater enthusiasm. And that's where Bruce wanted to be. Thus, Bruce had mixed feelings about starting this film. Was everything really ready? His doubts grew larger. He began coming down with physical ailments to delay shooting. We found it impossible to begin shooting with him.

So it was decided to shoot the scene with the praying mantises fighting to the death, anything to avoid pressuring Bruce to begin, but then the praying mantises wouldn't fight. It seemed no one wanted to start this film. Maybe they were suffering from jet lag since they had been flown in from the States. To make matters worse, there were no praying mantises available in Hong Kong. There was also another problem. Our Japanese cameraman, Nishimotosan, spoke no English. But worse, he didn't speak Chinese either. When I wanted to communicate with him I would have to tell my Chinese assistant, Chaplin Chang, who would tell a Chinese crewman who spoke Chinese and understood Japanese and he would then tell Nishimotosan. My God! Then, of course, the answer would come back through the same torturous route. By the time the praying mantises started fighting and eating one another, I knew we had to get a different cameraman.

There was a growing worry that Bruce would withdraw from the movie. Principal photography had been rescheduled once again when I got a late evening call from Linda informing me that Bruce was **not** going to make **Enter the Dragon**. Bruce wanted to meet and talk about it at a restaurant near the hotel. She told me Bruce was angry about a lot of things, but he was still feeling betrayed by Fred and Paul. To complicate matters, Warner Brothers sent Bruce another martial arts film script. Bruce decided to abort **Enter the Dragon** for the new script and wanted to send everyone home, though he asked me to stay on and direct the newest offering. I told him this was madness. He had to be talked out of it and that's what I set about doing. Too much money and effort had already been spent to be thrown aside at this late hour. Bruce had made up his mind, but little by little he came around. It was another long night.

Once again Bruce let real and imagined hurts hamper his better judgment. All he needed was someone to sit down with him and quietly review the problem. Almost always, it was Linda who filled this role. She kept him from going "too far" on many occasions. She was very important to Bruce, but she never played the dreaded "star's wife." She gave Bruce confidence and calmed him when he was at his most volatile. Still, **Enter the Dragon** came very close to being canceled.

John Saxon arrived in Hong Kong with a negative attitude about the entire production, having stated earlier at Warner Brothers that he assumed he had been hired to "give the film some class." "I mean," Andre Morgan said, "he came out thinking that he was the real star of the piece."

The reality was that Saxon was very standoffish when he got to Hong Kong and his wife hated the city. She virtually refused to eat Chinese food. Raymond Chow hosted a dinner party for the Saxons, along with several others of the American contingent, at a very nice restaurant. The next day, Andre innocently asked how the dinner went and

Raymond said, 'Ahhhh! It was a disaster!' Then Raymond told Andre what happened. "It was upstairs in the private dining room and we were all drinking Shaoshing wine and you know how they heat the wine and serve it in a teapot. Well, John Saxon's wife hated every course and didn't want to eat anything. I was getting anxious and the only thing I could think of was to keep pouring wine. I thought if everybody was a little drunk it would be better. We **finally** got to the end of the meal and Mrs. Saxon had hardly eaten three bites, but she was drinking the Shaoshing. So I reached over and took the teapot and swirled it around and offered her some more wine, which she agreed to have, but when I poured it I realized that I poured a cockroach into her cup. And, yes, she saw it, and yes, I thought she was going to die. Nothing worked well last night."

In the midst of the confusion, Fred and I received a dinner invitation to Sir Run Run's palatial home built on his studio grounds. Though we would be consorting with Raymond Chow's mortal enemy, it would be foolish to refuse.

We arrived at the Shaw Brothers Studios in a chauffeur-driven limousine. Our driver was waved through the high gates and directed toward the house at the end of a lengthy circular driveway. Along with other strategic positions, the driveway was protected by armed guards carrying automatic weapons. Dressed in studio uniforms, they were all alert to the possibility of kidnapping. (We were later told a couple members of his family had been kidnapped over the years.)

At dinner, we met Sir Run Run's favorite nephew, Vee King. He was being groomed as a possible heir to the Shaw Brothers empire. This was the young man who had been kidnapped a couple of years before, but had managed to escape from a locked automobile trunk, saving Sir Run Run from paying a large ransom. To save money is to be honored by the old man.

The dinner was held in an elegant dining room at a long table which seated 14. Sir Run Run sat at the head of the table with his wife, Lily, at the other end. At one side sat Sir Run Run's mistress, Mona Fong. Things are done much differently on that side of the world. Actor William Holden was also invited to dinner. He tried to convince Sir Run Run to finance a film from the book **Tai Pan**. The film project was eventually done much later with different people and disastrous results.

A British film censor who sat nearby spoke with high purpose about how he was safeguarding the morals of the Chinese people with his diligent censorship. His argument might have been better received if his fingernails hadn't been so filthy.

After dinner the party broke into small groups. It was then that Fred and I found out why we'd been invited to dinner. Sir Run Run's son, Vee Ming, paired off with Fred. The valued nephew, Vee King, mingled with me. Through cigar smoke, an interrogation began. What did we think of Bruce Lee? Was he a true star? Yes? Would he continue to be a leading man? What was the budget of **Enter the Dragon**? What did we think it would ultimately cost? Would it ever be finished? Did the Chinese and American crews get along?

Bruce Lee was injured several times during the filming of *Enter the Dragon*, including one cut on his hand that required 12 stitches to close. Still, he was a tireless worker, agreeing to shoot a scene as many as a dozen times if it meant getting it right.

We were told later Sir Run Run did not have many social dinners. He always ended up grilling his guests.

Many do not understand how physically demanding the making of an action film can be on the principal players, especially when there are no doubles. There were fight scenes that required Bruce to dispose of a dozen attackers, all of it in one "take." There was no way that a double could be used, or even used in rehearsals, because the timing had to be perfected by Bruce himself, who ultimately had to run it for the camera.

Each of these dozen adversaries had to kick or hit precisely in rapid succession or it would look fake to the audience. There is nothing worse than an attacker flying backward or being lifted off the ground when it is obvious he has not been hit. Now, here is Bruce kicking out side to side, front to back, as the fighters are fed into the fray, and each of these 12 men must be in the right place at the right time and react properly. If **one** misses his mark, or stumbles, or if Bruce misses **one** of those 12, even if only by an inch (and you can imagine them all turning and twisting and jumping in and out), the scene has to be reset. Any single take is strenuous, though not so much for the dozen attackers, any of which has but one thing to do, but for Bruce, who has 12 pieces of action to think about, as well as portraying the proper expression and attitude. Some fight scenes required as many as 14 takes. This requires enormous energy and endurance from the principal. There was no way for Bruce to judge if a take was good. He might say it "felt" good, but only the director and a stuntman standing close by the camera can make that judgment. Not even the cameraman, who's looking through a very small viewfinder, can be sure. Then there's always the decision to rest everyone or quickly move on while everyone is "hot." All this drained Bruce at a great rate, yet he never asked for a break, nor did he complain, even after the tenth take when a fighter made

his move too soon or reacted too late. No director could ask any more from a performer.

Bruce was injured several times during the picture and many who had known him for years said he did not look well. They spoke of his weight loss and his skin tone (some said he had grown darker, while others thought he looked pale.) He told of many sleepless nights, during which he would draw his unique stick figures in "film battle," choreographing fight scenes on paper.

During the filming of **Enter the Dragon**, Sir Run Run was keeping a close eye on the Golden Harvest project. It was rumored he had informers at every level of production. He publicly stated he believed the film would never be completed. Privately he hoped it would be a disaster. He finally came to realize his mortal enemy, Raymond Chow, had pulled off a major coup by making the first international picture in Hong Kong. Sir Run Run started mulling this over. He decided to gear up the Shaw Brothers Studios to do what Raymond had done—make co-production deals with foreign companies, particularly American film companies. He made five international films in quick succesion including **Cleopatra Jones and the Casino of Gold** with Warner Brothers. He wanted to show that his company was better than the outfit down the road. However, they all failed, one after the other. Raymond was getting too big for Sir Run Run to squash. Plus, Golden Harvest was building its own distribution network that has now become the biggest in Asia, displacing Shaw Brothers.

There is a fundamental difference in the way Americans, and in particular the American film community, see martial arts and martial arts films, and the way the Chinese judge both. The martial arts have been a part of the Chinese culture and heritage for thousands of years. It is a very real part of their lives. Every morning you can see young and old people practicing tai chi chuan in any Hong Kong park. Most Americans and Europeans see all this as a fantasy, especially when viewed on screen. The Chinese felt the primary location, Han's Island, was an impossibility. And, indeed, **Han** was an impossibility. Many of the weapons and uniforms used offended the Chinese purists. However, it didn't "read" wrong to Westerners because they don't know the difference. If a Chinese film company came to the United States and made a "Western" and put cowboy characters in tai silk shirts and soft slippers, we would be offended, or angry, or simply dismiss it as a stupid joke. **Enter the Dragon** bothered quite a number of Chinese in the same way.

Bruce often met with the stuntmen at night after shooting. His presence would draw a circle of waiters and cooks from the kitchen. They would prepare his favorite noodles and barbecued pork. It was more than just camaraderie as many men were more or less on Bruce's payroll. He saw to many of their needs and they were on his team. Some would need loans and he was as generous to them as he was to so many others. Though they were not professional bodyguards, they certainly would have taken care of any threat to Bruce's life. They were tough, loyal and dependent in some ways. It was not easy being a stuntman in Hong Kong. They risked life and limb without the technology or expensive equipment taken for granted in Hollywood. There was no breakaway glass or airbags to break falls. They always seemed to be limping around.

The stuntmen belonged to one of the many factions of Triads, the Chinese Mafia-like organization. It is one large group, but within that group are individual "families," each competing with the other. When we needed more stuntmen than one family could supply, we would have to call in the

stuntmen from rival families, which led to near mortal fights. In any of the mass fights, such as the climactic encounter on the tournament field, the staged fight would quickly degenerate into a vengeful brawl. The fights did not necessarily stop when I yelled "cut." In fact, the stage battle was just another excuse to maim one another. It was a cover and screen to the bloodletting that occurred on a daily basis in Hong Kong.

At times there were as many as 400 extras in the tournament scenes. Many of them belonged to rival street gangs. Confrontations staged for the camera often broke into real battles. Many of these young men were poor with little to look forward to in their lives. Bruce used to sit among these men when he wasn't needed in a scene. As he practiced his moves and kicks, the extras would lie on the grass, much of which had to be painted green, or sit on top of the walls. Sometimes one of the men would decide to challenge Bruce. The classic challenge was to tap your foot three times in front of Bruce. For the most part Bruce would laugh it off. A few would persist by becoming increasingly insulting. They would insinuate Bruce was nowhere as good as he was said to be.

Putting aside his beloved chrysanthemum tea, Bruce would eventually call over the loud one. Bruce would never begin the encounter, but would ask the fellow if he knew anything about jeet kune do. The fighter would grin back at his buddies and say that he knew as much as he needed to know. The man would kick out, though Bruce would not move as the kick would invariably fall short. Then Bruce would lash out two or three times in rapid succession, not trying to kill him, but to "mark" him. Draw blood, as it were. One of these fellows did not seem to have a mark on him after this exchange until he opened his mouth to reveal an avalanche of blood.

Chapter Fourteen

Death Wish

Bruce had another run-in with one of the film's cast members. Bruce's fight scene with Bob Wall was all too real. In one scene, Bruce was supposed to kill Bob to avenge the death of his sister, who was played by Angela Mao. In the first part of this scene, Bruce kicked Bob over a row of folding chairs and through a line of Han's cadre. Bob picked up two bottles that were supposed to hold water for the contestants. He smashed the bottles together and advanced toward Bruce with a broken bottle in each hand. This was real glass since there were no breakaway bottles available in Hong Kong. As Bob got close, Bruce was to spin around, kick a bottle out of his hand and Bob was to drop the bottle. Bruce would then spin around a second time and club Bob with his fist. Everyone knew how precise Bruce was with this sort of action. The scene was rehearsed a couple of times and then we rolled.

Bob stepped forward and Bruce began to spin. Bruce kicked within a fraction of Bob's hand, but Bob kept hold of the bottle. Later he said Bruce missed his target so he thought he should hang on to the bottle. But Bruce followed with his second spin. Bruce hit the edge of the broken bottle with his hand and needed 12 stitches to close the cut on his finger. Chaplin Chang, the assistant

"Bruce had to save face. He had to kill Bob Wall."

Enter the Dragon acted as much as a training ground for its principals as it did a springboard for its star. Bob Wall, Jim Kelly and John Saxon trained extensively with Bruce Lee.

director, took Bruce to the hospital. "He was bleeding worse than people were told. Blood was on the car seats." He wouldn't be able to work for a couple days.

Meanwhile, the stuntmen were starting to grumble. They began to say Bob deliberately tried to hurt Bruce. They met with Bruce that night in a Kowloon cafe and Bruce got caught up in their accusations. Bruce had stated on several occasions that Bob was not a friend of his and he had even expressed outright antagonism toward the actor. A couple of days later, I got a call from Raymond who said Bruce was in a fury. Bruce had been meeting with his stuntmen and agreed to exact revenge for this treacherous act. Now they were all high on the idea and there was no turning back. Bruce had to

save face. Raymond said I had to figure a way out. We were to reshoot the scene with the bottles and then finish the fight. Bruce was to make a run at Bob and come flying at him with a kick in the chest. Bruce told Raymond this was to be it. By breakfast I had come up with the answer. On the set, I told Bruce I had heard he meant to do Bob in. Bruce grimly nodded. I told him we needed Bob for scenes to be shot in the States. Bob had to stay healthy for the good of the picture. Actually, everything in the States was already in the can so I was lying. Bruce stared at me a couple seconds and finally started to nod. He reluctantly agreed. He went to his guys, who were all huddled together and waiting for the kill, and told them the director would not allow it. Bob had

Bruce Lee is listed in *Enter the Dragon* as the chief fight choreographer, but in reality he was much more. The film revolved around him and he took an active interest in every portion of the decision-making process.

to live for the good of the picture. Bruce was probably relieved to get out of the situation. He had to have a way of saving face.

We all developed a great deal of respect for the Chinese people after working under such horrendous conditions. There was very little budget for set construction and props for **Enter the Dragon**. Everyone had to make do. For instance, we needed the look of steel bars for the prison cells in the dungeon set. In Hollywood the construction people had dowel cut to length and had them sprayed black by the paint department. Not so at Golden Harvest. Someone had to go through a pile of scrap boards behind the stage to find lengths that were close to two-by-two. He then laid out a long board and nailed notched blocks of wood on both ends. Now he could lay the two-by-two into these notches and run down its entire length with a small plane to remove a thin ribbon of wood. Then he would turn the two-by-two a little and pull the plane down the length again. He did this over and over until he had created a round bar some eight feet long. Laborious yet cheaper than buying dowel!

The dungeons on the set of **Enter the Dragon** were made of mud. Buckets upon buckets of mud were brought onto the stage by elderly women and smeared on wooden frames and chicken wire. As the mud dried it began to crack and crumble on the floor. We couldn't shoot certain angles, and fights had to be staged to avoid having bodies smashed against the walls. We had to hurry and finish the last scenes before the whole thing collapsed. The extras who filled in the prison cells in our dungeon were found on the streets of Hong Kong. They were mostly drunks and vagrants. As I moved among them, staging shots, they mumbled in slurred Chinese. Chaplin, the first assistant director, was following behind, shaking his head. I asked him what was going on and he said, "I'm embarrassed to tell what they are suggesting they want to do to you. In fact, I won't tell you."

Bruce meant many things to millions of people, but he was also a source of income for film crews, actors, stuntmen and producers. The studio protected him the way a trainer would protect a thoroughbred. Every time Bruce "left the gate" he brought in millions. Golden Harvest could invest and plan other productions based on his predicted future earnings. A Bruce Lee can generate money far beyond his films alone. His work lifted the Hong Kong film industry to a much higher level and made its products more acceptable to the world. Bruce stimulated the sale of newspapers, magazines, T-shirts, posters, toys, candy bars and popcorn. But more important, he brought joy to an enormous and worshipful worldwide audience.

One of the major highlights of the film was the mirrored-room sequence, which was not in the original script. The room was completely faced with mirrors and a smaller room. A box of about six feet square and eight feet high was built and placed in the center of the room. This also was covered with mirrors. No matter where you were standing, reflections were reflecting reflections. In one wall of the larger room, three shallow bays about five feet wide were constructed. These bays were lined with narrow mirrors running vertically and forming a concave depression. These narrow mirrors broke up any image into a dozen images. It was startling to see a figure walk in front of the mirrors. Then a baffle of plywood about three feet wide and five feet high was built and faced with mirrors with a hole cut for the lens of the camera. This allowed us to be in the room without being seen by simply adding another reflecting surface. The total cost of the mirrors was $8,000—another expense that had not been figured in.

"We had two truck loads of mirrors," Andre said. "The glass company couldn't believe it." Using a director's finder I moved slowly in the room, turning this way and that, and positioned Chaplin and his guy in

various positions. I had them walk here and there and one stuck a piece of tape on the floor and marked it. Amazing visual things were happening. It got more and more exciting. I finally had the two guys playing Bruce and (villain) Shih Kien and throwing punches and kicks. When I showed Bruce the mirrored room, he was interested but not too excited. What I told him next made him upset for the first time in the production—at least with me. I lined him up in front of Shih Kien, only six inches from his face. I told Bruce he had to kick him in the head, or rather look as if he kicked him in the head. Bruce looked at me and Shih Kien and then started to shake his head.

"That's ridiculous," he said. "My foot will be three feet behind his head! I'll look stupid!" "Yes, it will be three feet behind him," I told Bruce. "But it won't be in the mirrors."

It took awhile to explain. He was finally convinced and willing to try it. The crew shot for two days. It was the last two days of the film and the city was experiencing a heat wave. Paul Heller tried to find electric fans, but it was not a success. The studio had no air conditioning. The dailies for both days were seen the day the crew was to leave for Los Angeles. Both Bruce and Raymond were in the screening room and Bruce went crazy. The dailies were so sensational that after the crew left Hong Kong, Bruce got a Golden Harvest crew together and shot in the mirrored room for two weeks on his own.

Toward the end of filming, Bruce and I were approaching complete exhaustion. After one particularly difficult day of shooting, Bruce came up to me and said rather bitterly, "There are only two people who give a damn what this picture looks like—you and me."

As we were in the final stage of editing at Warner Brothers, an executive came in to say the picture was a year too late. He said there were too many martial arts films around and the craze had died. Executives love to make these sweeping statements and they're so often wrong. **Enter the Dragon** was an immediate success; but what marvels experts has been its amazing staying power. It continues to play everywhere in the world year after year. It still plays on network television in the United States. Interestingly, it did not do as well in Hong Kong as Bruce's other pictures. Some feel the Chinese were in love with Bruce being a country bumpkin and they didn't appreciate his Western transformation. Except for Japan, the film grossed less in Asia than his other works. The worldwide theatrical gross at the time of this writing is $150 million. Considering the ratio of money invested to money earned, it has to be one of the most profitable pictures ever made.

Raymond Chow had never released Bruce's other films in Japan because the Japanese would never accept a Chinese star. But with **Enter the Dragon** selling even bigger than it did in America, Raymond released all to further high grosses.

The producers were thinking of going back to the **Blood and Steel** title or maybe even a new title—**Han's Island**. Bruce was told he had better defend the title or it was going to be dropped. He sent a wire to Ted Ashley at Warner Brothers saying if the title was changed he'd never make another picture for them again. They quickly backed off.

Chapter Fifteen

A Time To Live

For the first time in his life, Bruce felt free to splurge without a sense of guilt. From London, he ordered a gold colored Rolls Royce Corniche. It was to be delivered in six months, but the order was soon to be canceled.

Linda said that Bruce, in April following the conclusion of photography for **Enter the Dragon**, had made up his mind to go back to California as soon as possible. He would only return to Hong Kong for an occasional picture. But on May 10, 1973, Linda said, "My world fell apart."

The occurrences of May 10 are vital to understanding what happened a little more than three months later—the day Bruce died. It was a virtual rehearsal of his death, a grim preview if you will. Statements from the doctors about the May 10 incident are from the coroner's inquest held about four months after Bruce's fatal attack, July 20, 1973. Most of the medical opinion was given in a public hearing from Dr. Charles Langford, an American practicing at Baptist Hospital, and Dr. Peter Woo, a Chinese neurosurgeon, along with the testimony from Raymond Chow and others.

Friday, May 10, 1973 was a typical Hong Kong day—hot and sweltering. It was typhoon weather. Bruce had been "looping" lines for **Enter the Dragon** on a poorly air-

"I have the body of an 18-year-old."

conditioned stage at the top of Hammerhill Road. The air conditioning would not have been running anyway, since its noise would have been picked up by the recording equipment. These ancient Cathay Studio buildings failed to have proper roof ventilation. And Bruce had not yet fully recovered from the energy drain caused by the film's schedule. Looking wan and exhausted, Bruce left the stage for the men's lavatory, where, we now know, he was trying to clear his head. Instead, he collapsed on the restroom floor. He later told Linda he believes he did not lose consciousness and when he heard footsteps coming in his direction he struggled on the floor, pretending to have dropped his glasses. Even now, in this threatening condition, Bruce could not admit to a weakness or flaw. Yet, it is reasoned, he must have fainted because the crew did not start checking on him for 15 or 20 minutes, and Bruce felt he had hardly been in the restroom any length of time. In any case, he got up from the floor and started out, or so Bruce believes. A crewman says he helped Bruce stand and then watched him walk unsteadily out of the restroom. He made his way onto the stage, ready to begin work again, and then collapsed. This time he **was** unconscious and convulsions began to wrack his body. He threw up.

Raymond Chow was called and quickly came to the stage, urgently asking for someone to call nearby Baptist Hospital. Chow found that Bruce was "having difficulty breathing. He was making a loud noise and was shaking." Dr. Langford told people at the studio to bring him to the hospital as quickly as possible. The doctor was waiting when they arrived and he immediately conducted an examination that showed that Bruce was suffering from a high fever and did not consciously respond to stimuli.

Dr. Langford testified that, "Lee was brought in by several men from the studio. First there were breathing noises, then they stopped. There was a series of convulsions.

Three other doctors were summoned, including a neurosurgeon, Dr. Peter Woo. Lee was going through muscle contraction and relaxation. The entire body was involved in this motion, but the upper limbs gave us most difficulty because he was very strong and was difficult to control. After the failure of Mr. Lee to respond for a period, and after waiting for the neurosurgeon to examine him, we gave him drugs to reduce the swelling of the brain which we had detected."

Dr. Woo, in turn, testified that Lee's eyes were moving to the right and left in a circular motion after he was revived, and that his speech was slurred.

Later, in July, Dr. Langford was asked by the coroner if this attack could have been brought about by exhaustion. The doctor said no.

Dr. Langford also testified that, "It was quite dramatic when he regained consciousness. First he was able to move a bit, then he opened his eyes, then he made some sign, but could not speak. He recognized his wife and made signs of recognition, but he could not talk. Later he was able to speak, but it was slurred, different from the usual way he talked. By the time he was transferred to another hospital, he was able to remember aloud and joke."

Both doctors agreed that Bruce had been very close to death.

Plans had been made for Bruce and Linda to fly to New York for appearances on several television shows, including "The Tonight Show" with Johnny Carson. At the same time, Bruce was weighing offers from around the world, with Warners' bid of a million dollars for this next picture among the highest. Very few stars, even American personalities, were being offered those figures in 1973. Producer Carlo Ponti, from Rome, wanted Bruce to star with his wife, Sophia Loren, for a large sum that was "to be determined." Bruce was free to accept any offer; he was not committed to Golden Harvest or his own company, Concord. He

Although there were moments of levity on the set of *Enter the Dragon*, they were few and far between. The constant drain on Bruce Lee's energy caused him to grow pale and lose weight. No one knew it at the time, but it marked the beginning of the end of Bruce Lee's life.

flew to California for a couple more days of looping at Warner Brothers, and then admitted himself into the UCLA Medical Center, where a series of tests were to be conducted, all of it based on testimony and information released following his May 10 collapse.

The examination was handled, primarily, by Dr. David Reisbord. Bruce was given a complete physical, though there was considerable time spent on brain tests. The tests were exhaustive, but the doctors could not find any sign of the previous attack, nor any impending problem. The stress-related "time bomb" that lurked in Bruce's brain had healed itself sufficiently to avoid detection, yet the weakness remained, hidden. He was declared fit and told he had the body of an 18-year-old.

Following the tests, Bruce went to Warner Brothers for a screening of **Enter the Dragon** in its nearly finished form. There was no music and no fades or dissolves, nor had any other optical work been done. The "work print" was marred with scratches and the editor's grease pencil marks and was run with a separate soundtrack that did not include sound effects that were still being prepared. Bruce, who sat next to me at the screening, did not need a finished or "answer print" to know what a winner was when he saw it. He looked at me for a couple seconds and then said, grinning, "We've got it." He knew the world was his for the taking and returned to Hong Kong with soaring spirits.

But Bruce could not be content for long and soon he was working on further additions to **The Game of Death**. He was more temperamentally suited to wage war than deal with victory. He could not handle peace.

Bruce was becoming more and more withdrawn and there are indications of paranoia in his dealings with people. He had never before had to handle success. This was a true test.

No matter where a film is being made,

Assuming a kung-fu hand position, Bruce Lee stands in the makeshift area which became Han's courtyard in *Enter the Dragon*.

information about a project can be rapidly trammitted. The easy flow of conversation between artists and executives by transcontinental telephone, and through a million daily lunches, late-night parties and bar talk, starts the process toward a consensus of any given production. When a film is in trouble or going over budget, or if a particular picture has the potential of "flying," it is soon known. The word of winners and losers seeps through the cracks of editorial rooms, music sessions and sound-mixing studios. A collective knowledge builds until an opinion has been gained. People will nod when a certain name or title is mentioned, though it may be unknown to the public for the moment. Yes, we know. Yes, I've heard the same thing.

Yes. Future deals are proposed based on what will surely be, and no one wants to miss the boat. So it was with **Enter the Dragon**. Warner executives were ecstatic with what they had seen, even before Lalo Schifrin wrote the music. Producer Paul Heller said, "They went bananas." Studio publicity men had been alerted and the foreign sales chief, Richard Ma, and distribution head, Leo Greenfield, were gearing up their departments. This was going to be a big one and, indeed, only **The Exorcist** outgrossed it in 1973, though the film had not been released until August.

The word was being heard in London and Rome and New York. Long idle projects that were "perfect" for Bruce were being

resurrected. Offers began to reach Bruce in growing numbers and he was pleased and bewildered by the attention. Still, he continued to grow cautious and suspicious.

Many entertainers have lengthy professional lives and an arm's-length list of credits and accomplishments. The Bob Hopes and Frank Sinatras have been around for more than 50 years, but for Bruce it was crammed into six hectic years. Bruce only appeared as a leading man in four films (not counting the small part in the non-completed **The Game of Death**.) One can only speculate on what Bruce might have done, or how far he might have gone had he lived a full life. He had been receiving dozens of offers from every film capital in the world, all of them shaking bundles of money before his eyes, and Bruce was coming to realize what power an international celebrity has and how it can be used if he is willing to be used. Like many a star before him, he began to shy from those he felt he could not trust, and the list grew as a near paranoia began to envelop him. Bruce's actor friend, Thomas Chan, said that Bruce had told him, "I have money in front of me that is like a mountain. There is so much of it. This money is there if I want to reach out for it. But I must be very, very careful because the people who want me to have this money want to own me. I must be very careful." Chan goes on, "He did not want to be used and he did not have a real friend. In his whole life he did not have a real friend. The last two years he was in Hong Kong he was lonely, very lonely." Chan obviously was not aware of Bruce's friendship with Taky Kimura and James Lee in the United States.

Bruce Lee, *Enter the Dragon* producer Fred Weintraub and Linda Lee share a lighter moment during the banquet scene. At about this time, Bruce was such a big star his name was plastered over the pages of every Hong Kong newspaper. This caused many problems because Bruce was being linked to every Hong Kong starlet.

Chapter Sixteen

Honeymoon's Over

Bruce agreed to appear at the Shaw Studios for elaborate costume fittings and ancient hair stylings to run screen tests for a period picture featuring Nin Kang Yiu, a hero of Chinese history. He did this to raise the anxiety level of Golden Harvest executives. It succeeded. Bruce had no intention of leaving Golden Harvest, but he knew how to play a pressure game. Conversely, other pressure points were being used against him. Independent producers were offering $10,000 to Bruce's friends if they could get his signature on a contract. This set off a fierce competition for Bruce's attention.

He could not go out in public without being mobbed by the tens of thousands of fans who only wanted to touch him. He started going to dinner with Charles Lowe, who had been the second cameraman on **Enter the Dragon** and was building a reputation for quality camera work. Bruce liked Japanese food, particularly sashimi, which is raw fish. Lowe and Bruce would go to a Japanese restaurant in Kowloon called Kanetanaka, where he could find some relief in a private room. Even here the shoji screen would often slide open and the heads of waitresses could be seen bobbing about, trying to gain a glimpse of Bruce or sending in batches of cardboard coasters to be autographed. Bruce had started to drink,

"I don't know how long I can keep this up."

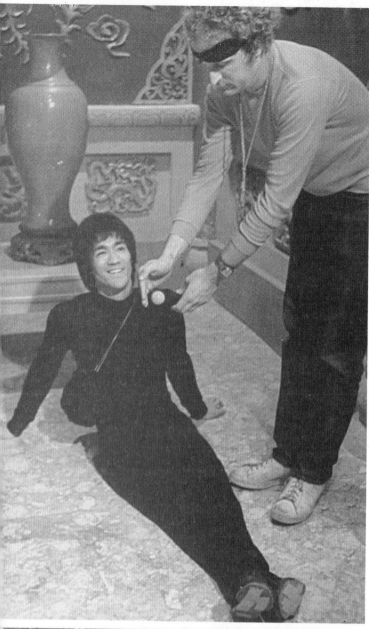

which he had seldom done before these last days. "He could really drink saki," Lowe said. "We met for dinner many, many times, and he would drink 10 or 20 of these ceramic bottles of saki in an evening."

Near the end he was consuming large amounts of a drink called "wei-ta-nai" which is the juice squeezed from the "dou jiang" bean. Charles Lowe tells of Bruce refusing water, but drinking copious amounts of "wei-ta-nai." Lowe felt this juice, in great amounts, was bad for Bruce, but Bruce insisted that it gave him strength. Yet, Lowe noted, he was very tired and dizzy much of the time and that his complexion was poor. "We Chinese," Lowe said, "make much of a person's complexion. Bruce was very pale and his skin did not shine."

Bruce would tell Lowe of the many offers he was receiving, but that he did not think he wanted to make more than two more pictures as an actor, and neither picture would be of the martial arts genre. He told Lowe he was being besieged by people who would tell him they were his uncle's best friend, or his teacher's old friend or pupil, and they would ask if he could get them into the film business or lend them money. So many were trying to get close to him, all wearing the same fixed smile Bruce had come to loathe. He told Lowe he could talk to him without fear of being asked for something or having a "deal" presented to him. They could talk about things that they wanted to do in the future, or talk about cameras and lenses, which interested Bruce. They would finish dinner in a couple of hours and then separate, with Bruce usually going to one of three places—home and to his family, Betty Ting Pei's apartment, where occasionally Raymond Chow would meet him, or the studio. Bruce had never slept much and now he found himself even more restless.

Bruce was obviously going headlong in two directions. One moment he could tell Linda, "There is no limit, no end in sight, to how far I can ascend in my knowledge of

Bruce Lee was a favorite of the everyday Chinese film worker. Rather than eat with the executives, he chose to dine with the stuntmen and crew. They would have done anything for him. In turn, he helped make working conditions and pay better for those behind the scenes.

acting and the martial arts," and in the next announce, "I don't know how long I can keep this up." Events were beginning to dictate an ever-increasing pace, exaggerating a lifetime of running at a fever rate.

The honeymoon between Bruce and the Hong Kong press had long since passed. The insatiable public appetite for any news about Bruce finally caused the well of information to run dry. His life, as busy and raucous as it was, could not supply the many tabloids with daily stories. To relieve this bottleneck, many newspapers put their more creative, and vindictive, reporters to work **producing** Bruce Lee stories. They either concocted stories **entirely** from their own fertile minds or created large exposes based on scraps of information.

Had Bruce been 20 minutes late getting to the studio this morning?! If so, why? They conjured reasons for this alarming occurrence. He had gotten home late the night before? Which actresses could have kept Bruce out all night and thus made him 20 minutes late for work? Nora Miao was in Taiwan, but Betty Ting Pei was available, right there in her apartment in Kowloon Tong and only a 15-minute walk for Bruce.

Some stories were so raunchy that Bruce sought legal recourse, but he died before any of the cases could be heard in court.

When Bruce died the newspapers went berserk: The story carried so many ramifications reporters hardly knew where to begin. That he was a superstar dead at 32 was news enough, but then there was the matter of the

173

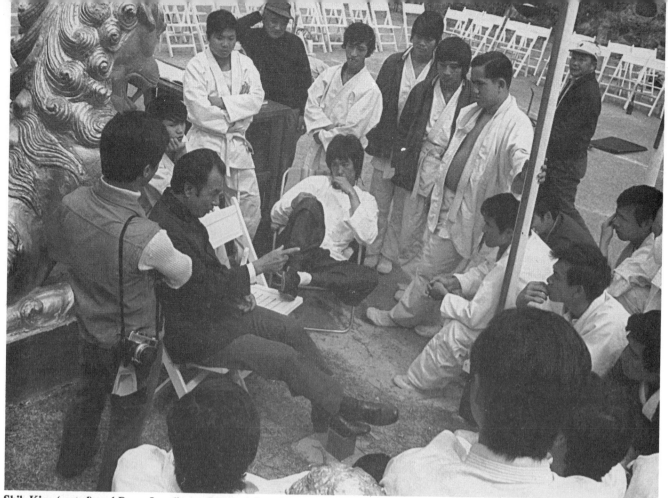

Shih Kien (seated) and Bruce Lee discuss fight logistics with many of the extras who would be involved in the courtyard fight scene. The majority of extras were gang members pulled from the Hong Kong streets.

death itself. That alone was a big story. Where he died was just as significant. There was the studio's attempt to hide pertinent facts. There were all sorts of wild stories about the cause of death. If it had been murder, speculation ran rampant. Was it: the Triads, a jealous mistress, a disgruntled martial arts master, drug dealers, a raging Run Run Shaw, the invisible hand, spurned film producers, or Raymond Chow himself. Or the dreaded "vibrating palm." Or vengeful Shaolin priests. Or all of these in concert and conspiracy! One rumor had Bruce, a knapsack over his shoulder, heading for seclusion deep into the China hills. They believed he would return like a messiah in a few years. The body in Betty Ting Pei's apartment belonged to somebody else, of course.

Many recalled an instance, not long before he died, when Bruce's frustrations boiled over. The cause was his former director, and perceived enemy, Lo Wei. After **Enter the Dragon**, Raymond Chow had invited Lo Wei out to lunch where he asked him about a picture from Cambodia called **Snake Girl** that was making very big money. Raymond asked him to view the film, which they had at the studio, and to suggest the reasons for its success. They went back to the studio and Lo and his wife and Leonard Ho, Raymond's partner, and upcoming executive Andre Morgan, joined Lo on his way to the screening room, with Raymond going into his office. Lo saw Bruce behind a window curtain, but he showed no recognition. Linda related in her book that Bruce was at the studio discussing ideas with Raymond Chow for the ongoing film **The Game of Death**, when he heard that Lo was in a screening room. Lo Wei represented all that Bruce felt was rotten with Mandarin films and his temper erupted. He rushed down to the screening room and in a loud

Shih Kien, who played the villain "Han," Bruce Lee and John Saxon take a brief respite from filming to discuss camera angles and fight choreography.

voice told Lo what he thought of him. Satisfied at having vented his feelings, he returned to Chow's office.

What does Lo Wei remember of the encounter? "Halfway through the screening, suddenly, the door to the room opened and a man came to stand over me. It was dark and at first I could not see clear. Once clear, it was him. Two eyes open wide, arms akimbo, facing me. I did not say a word. I realized he was looking for trouble. First, I am older. Second, I do not know how to fight. Then he shouted at me, 'Yi kuan chin sho!' which means 'beast in human clothes.' I did not refute him because if I reply I would suffer. I did not make a sound, but continued to watch the film. Actually, deep inside me, I was scared because I could not fight him. I could not overcome him. Leonard Ho and my wife were scared, too, because of what might happen. He stared at me with two big eyes, arms akimbo. After awhile some people came

and dragged him out. Even though he was dragged out we were too scared to leave, so we continued to watch the film."

Back to Linda's account of the growing problem. "Bruce had returned to Raymond's office, but in maybe ten minutes Lo Wei's wife appeared and tempers again became heated and a considerable crowd had gathered. Mrs. Lo went back to her husband, leaving Bruce boiling over with anger and frustration. Under normal conditions, he would have quickly calmed down. Instead, he charged back to the screening room and gave Lo Wei another piece of his mind. The director claimed that Bruce had threatened him physically. An absurd claim, of course, but one which was bound to elicit both sympathy and publicity. The police were called and were followed by a horde of reporters. Lo Wei demanded that Bruce sign a paper promising not to harm him physically. Bruce, annoyed and upset by the whole incident and anxious to get the reporters off the premises, agreed to sign; later he could have kicked himself, for it appeared to incriminate him. Had Lo Wei been a young man and a reasonable match for him, Bruce's hot temper may well have found an outlet in a fight; but the idea that he would strike or physically injure an old man is beyond credibility."

Back to Lo Wei: "Within ten minutes he came again. Once in, he came straight to me, pointing at my nose. He said, 'What's so marvelous about you?' He took his belt off and pulled out the buckle, which was a knife. Maybe four inches long. He took the knife and pointed it at my chest, maybe inch away. I looked at the knife, where it was pointing, and knew it was not my heart if he stabbed through. I would not die right away. This put my mind more at ease. He said, 'Do you believe I can kill you with one stab?' I did not say a word. I smiled at him. At that moment Raymond Chow and many others came to push him out. With this incident, I could tolerate no more. After he was pushed out I got up and went to the telephone and tell the girl at the main switchboard to call the police, to call 999. The girl had already called 999. When others found out I had asked that, they said I should not have done that. I said I was tired of keeping my life safe from him. In a little while came a lot of police cars, police and inspectors. They talk in office first and then they come to me. At first it was absurd. Inspector asked me, 'Who dialed 999?' I said I did. He said, 'What happened?' I said that Bruce Lee had threatened me with a knife. He said, 'Good. You come with me to the police station.' It made me laugh. I said, 'Do you not have it clear? **I** am the victim! **I** am the accuser! You want me to go to the police station? Why do you not ask him to go?' He said, 'He has a lawyer.' I said, 'You do not mean to say that I do **not** have a lawyer?' Now they saw that the situation had become an impasse. Another inspector came over to 'turn the corner'

and smooth it out. He said, in fine-sounding tone, 'Mr. Lo, do not misunderstand. We searched for knife, but it had to have been thrown away. We cannot find. Now you are colleagues here, a small matter. Let it be.' I said I did not provoke him. I said I would not let it be! He said, 'Then what do you want?' I said I only want, in the future, that my life is not in danger. So the inspectors went to Bruce Lee. In the end he wrote a document that admitted his fault and saying that he did it impulsively and that he would never act this way toward director Wei again. They showed the piece of paper to me and I said I wanted one sentence added. What? I said I wanted him to add that if anything happened to me in the future and I am injured he could be held responsible. He did this and I left the studio."

By this time the press had arrived and Bruce was explaining the situation. He ridiculed the idea of having used a knife. "If I want to kill Lo Wei," he said, "I would not use a knife. Two fingers would be enough." The reporters appeared to sympathize with Lo Wei and Bruce was criticized by newspapers and cartoonists. He was cast as the unruly son acting disrespectfully toward an aging father. That night Bruce appeared on a television talk show. Linda speaks of the evening. "Bruce was asked to appear on Hong Kong TV that evening and the matter was raised again. Throughout his life Bruce had never feared to state openly and frankly how he felt about people or problems. He was never deliberately rude or deliberately ruthless. He was firm and straightforward, expressing his opinions clearly and unambiguously, which is very different. He did not attempt to conceal his dislike of Lo Wei or his methods, although at no time did he mention the man by his name. In an attempt to show how absurd were suggestions that he was prepared to use a weapon against Lo Wei, he decided to demonstrate a simple shoulder push on the interviewer, who was quite agreeable. Bruce put only a fraction of

Bruce Lee and director Robert Clouse, whom the star said was one of the few people to care about *Enter the Dragon*, measure distances for an upcoming fight scene.

the force he was capable of exerting into the demonstration, but it was still sufficient to look pretty fierce to viewers and next morning the papers, still seeking for sensation, built up the incident into more headlines. Bruce, in short, had become such a superstar that whatever he did was avidly seized on by the the local press. Inevitably, the picture that was presented was a distorted one. It was, very often, a part of the truth, but it was never the totality."

Again, Lo Wei painted a different picture. "Because of that unhappy incident, Raymond Chow took my former wife and myself to a movie that night and from there to 'siau yeh,' which is the local custom of a midnight meal. Raymond Chow phoned home from the restaurant to talk to Felicia, his wife, and she told him that she had seen Bruce on a television show with Ho Sho Sin and that he had scolded me and said that he would watch me die. A great many friends came to me, angry. But I was not injured and I said let it be. They said he also knocked the master of ceremonies down, but I did not see this for myself. Ten days later he was dead."